PROVOCATIVE ALLOYS: A POST-MEDIA ANTHOLOGY

EDITED BY
CLEMENS APPRICH, JOSEPHINE BERRY SLATER,
ANTHONY ILES & OLIVER LERONE SCHULTZ

Post-Media Lab & Mute Books

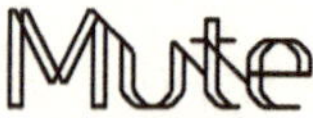

Co-published as a collaboration between Mute and the
Post-Media Lab, Leuphana University.
PML Books is a book series accompanying the work of the
Post-Media Lab. http://postmedialab.org

Print ISBN: 978-1-906496-94-4
Also available as eBook ISBN: 978-1-906496-95-1

Distribution Please contact mute@metamute.org for trade and distribution enquiries

Acknowledgements

Series Editors Clemens Apprich, Josephine Berry Slater, Anthony Iles &
Oliver Lerone Schultz
Layout Raquel Perez de Eulate
Design Template Based on a template by Atwork
Cover Image Artie Vierkant, *Image Objects*, 2011-present

PML Books

The first books in this short series are:

Felix Stalder, *Digital Solidarity*, (ISBN 978-1-906496-92-0)

Claire Fontaine, *Human Strike Has Already Begun & Other Writings*,
(ISBN 978-1-906496-88-3)

The PML Book series is just one of several outlets for the Lab's exploration of
post-media strategies and conditions, which includes fellowships, a virtual
lab structure, multiple collaborations, events, group readings and other
documentation.

For more information see: www.postmedialab.org/publications

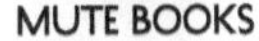

MUTE BOOKS

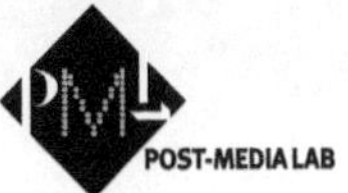

PML Books

The Post-Media Lab is part of the Lüneburg Innovation Incubator, a major EU
project within Leuphana University of Lüneburg, financed by the European
Regional Development Fund and co-funded by the German federal state of
Lower Saxony.

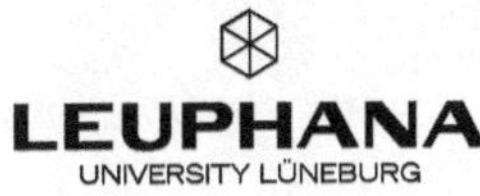

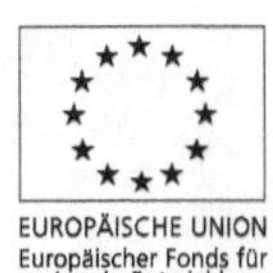

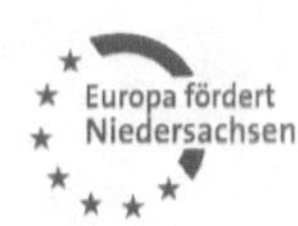

CONTENTS

PROVOCATIVE ALLOYS: AN INTRODUCTION

JOSEPHINE BERRY SLATER &
ANTHONY ILES

The Post-Media Lab was established in September 2011 as a collaboration between *Mute*, a culture and politics magazine based in London, and the Centre for Digital Cultures (CDC) at the Leuphana University of Lüneburg. The project picked up the diverse threads of different formulations of the experimental laboratory in media and net cultures, running from MIT's legendary Research Laboratory of Electronics (1946) to the small autonomous or semi-autonomous multimedia spaces which sprung up across Europe in the 1990s, like Vienna's Public Netbase/to, London's Backspace, Riga's E-Lab, Zagreb's MaMa and Ljubljana's Ljudmila. The Post-Media Lab aims to continue the experimental approaches of *Mute* and these labs, in their historically conscious and mongrelising use of media forms to upset uniform visions of the future. The Lab approaches the present conjunction of communications technology by looking both forwards and backwards, recognising the ways in which the past is not simply superceded but largely retained and reconfigured in the social and technological forms and relations of the present. This helps us begin to make sense of the fact that we live in a contradictory era of media monopolies *and* popular digital movements, Web 2.0 monocultures *and* cultural complexification, NSA *and* Anonymous. Following Félix Guattari, we call this struggle between molar and minor forms a 'post-media era'.

The Lab's focus on the potential of 'post-media' practice draws upon Guattari's concept of social and media assemblages which unleash new forms of collective expression and experience. It is centred around a supported programme of visiting fellows – artists, technologists, film-makers, curators, engineers, theorists and post-media operators – and the production of a series of associated, international public events and publishing projects. *Provocative Alloys: A Post-Media Anthology* forms part of a series of publications drawing on the Lab's two-year activities, and establishes the concept of 'post-media' in its historical development and contemporary relevance.

The period of the development of the internet through the 1990s and 2000s can be looked back upon as a period of acceleration, not only of technological developments and technical standards, but also of information, globalisation and capitalist expansion. Our moment – the second decade of the 21st century – represents the peak of this speed-up, galvanised by the globalisation of trade, governance and a truly world market. But the Lab setting provides not only the fuel for another acceleration, so-called creative 'innovation', but also the space in which to slow down, reflect upon the euphoria and damage of late capitalism, reintroduce history and tactically contemplate the current state of online commodification.

The term 'post-media' also acts as a placeholder for a series of historical retrievals that mark a specific moment and approach in radical culture. This entailed a shift in the late '90s and early 2000s from a net utopian perspective, to one that straddled both new media, offline social practices and older, even obsolete, media, eschewing any stable conformity to the disciplinary frameworks of art, politics or music. The blossoming of small and post-media initiatives in the rave, anarchist, small publishing and BBS scenes of the early '90s, as well as the alter-globalisation movement that they helped engender, provided a circulation of subversive and subterranean texts, media, music, political statements and events which increasingly seemed to speak to each other. The term 'post-media' provided a meeting point and catalyst for some of these diverse mileus of which *Mute* formed a part, in the '90s and the early-'00s, and the spirit of these times inspired the naming of the Lab. Drawing on Walter Benjamin's irrepressible proposition that 'nothing that has ever happened should be regarded as lost to history', the Lab was cultivated as a space that could provide respite from the tunnel-vision of relentless futurity, and establish the necessary process of reflection and activation through which any future must make the past its own concern.

Post-media's mixing of temporalities, forms and registers also extends to the selection of texts for this anthology which have been drawn from a range of cultural scenes. Adilkno's 'Theory of the Sovereign Media', from their 1998 *Media Archive,* is in any case a disparagement of mainstream media's attempts at an immediacy of representation. Their model of the sovereign media maker is, by contrast, that of a maker of messianic media whose activity, shunning the ubiquitous demand to connect and please, seeds the mediascape with time-chips indifferently awaiting their potential discovery. Howard Slater addresses Adilkno's media type in the title of his 'Post-Media Operators Sovereign and Vague' essay, published two years later in the underground zine *Datacide,* in which he considers it together with another of their categories, 'vague media'. In this piece, he contrasts the 'stopped flows' of mainstream journalism to the 'flawed and tentative' but singularly expressive productions of the post-media operator – an intermediary figure, analogous to Walter Benjamin's bricoleur. The post-media operator combines the faculties, sensibilities and distributive logic of activism, music, post-conceptual and media art into objects which flee from familiar perspectives and contexts. Her refusal of the linearity of current events combines an understanding of the present as specious with an experimental style of enunciation which doesn't depend on immediate audition, consumption or comprehension.

This dynamic of the critical retrieval of the past for the present is extended even further backwards by the inclusion of Michael Goddard's text which situates the development of Guattari's concept of post-media amidst the surreal-political enunciations of Bologna's Radio Alice. Goddard stresses the importance of the popular free radio movement for Guattari's concept of media assemblages and the critical importance of Italy as a model for politics in the 1970s. The short-lived station's dialogue with network culture is drawn out further via the figure of one of its key participants, media theorist, radio operator, and friend of Guattari, Franco 'Bifo' Berardi. A dialogue which Bifo continues to inject into media theory and politics to this day. Guattari's association of radio with the dynamics of polyvocality, de-specialisation, multi-directionality and hybrid combinations of technology, also find new resonances within contemporary net cultures and the social movements interwoven with them.

The singularities created by post-media practices can thus be related to the Romantic concept of history and art as based in self-reflection; social time comes to affect itself through producing a 'thinking of thinking', a consciousness of itself. This historical time is not only embedded in media assemblages as it is in all social artefacts, but can be unleashed by them, through the contingency of encounters. Creating diversions and folds in the feedback loops of history, which to a modest extent this anthology aims to perform, are a crucial part of the post-media thinking which forms the enunciative assemblages celebrated by Guattari. The fragment on its own can contain the condensation of a system – a gesture, intonation or modulation of syntax can do this too – and likewise the montage of fragments can unexpectedly expose a latent systemic relation. Post-media operators understand this, and in this way combine a work of singularisation with one of global analysis.

In Oliver Lerone Schultz's interview with media activists Felipe Fonseca (Brazil) and Alejo Duque (Colombia), the interaction between smallscale, autonomous practices and their deployment by the state is discussed. Lula's socialist government in Brazil turned to the expertise of urban media activists to try and implement its policy of digital inclusion for the country's often rural poor. The result was that some progressive ideas, such as copyleft and open source software, were integrated into government policy as ways to bridge chronic underdevelopment and the need to accelerate the use of computer networks. Although the activists had few illusions regarding the stakes of 'digital inclusion', nevertheless the experience of these delicate social and technical networks' use as conduits of increased normalisation was sobering. But, shifting their focus from the technical, Fonseca reports that the unexpected outcomes were the lessons media activists learned from poor communities in 'simple human values like generosity, sharing [and] dynamic social formations oriented to problem solving.' This exchange exemplifies the non-linearity of capitalist development and its resistance: pre-techncial networks of co-operation and enunciation come to affect a 'later' technical form that can be deployed to both normalising and singularising effect.

Post-media practice is an activity of searching for unexploited qualities inherent in exploitation; not a defiant negation as with the alternative media originated in the '60s, but a manipulation of manipulation. The trauma of mediatic envelopment can't be resolved by an exhumation or archaeology alone but, as with psychoanalysis, through the navigation of emergence. By contrast, site-specific art, which holds out the archaeological promise of producing meaning through digging into particularity, shows how easily this strategy gets subsumed into the homogeneity of place branding. Against this, Howard Slater understands post-media as avowedly immanent to the general equivalence of media forms, but nevertheless productive of self-evaluative warps which produce frictions and heteronomy out of this very condition.

It seems logical then that the post-media stance of producing seams or pockets of non-equivalence within a field of total equivalence has a natural affinity with ecological thinking which, of course, Guattari made explicit. The notion of 'ecologies' breaks down the transcendentalism of *the* environment into multiple milieus, while keeping in play their ultimate unity of interrelation. As Rasa Smite and Raitis Smits explain in their essay on the contemporary development of techno-ecological art, it is no wonder that new media artists, who once pioneered the exploration of the 'digital frontier', are attracted to working techno-ecologically. The net art of the '90s, defined by its 'process-based approach, collective creation and ability to establish (social) feedback', nevertheless operated within a technical system running on binary code and open (as in universally applicable) standards – the *élan vital* of the net. As post-media operators, first wave net artists were concerned to think singularity and universality at once, or, to think the production of non-equivalence within a field of globally expanding economic and technical equivalence. Peter Weibel, whom Smite and Smits quote, moves this idea on again, arguing that post-media art entails both 'equivalence of media' and the 'mixing of media' which entails the convergence of all media through digital computation and its effect on the sovereignty of each media form. In Weibel's words:

> Hence painting has come to life not by virtue of itself, but through its referencing of other media. Video lives from film, film lives from literature, and sculpture lives from photography and video.

With both art and ecology, a certain unity of conditions (binary code / total volume of carbon dioxide levels in the Earth's atmosphere) are dialectically tied to the production of local conditions or expressions which oscillate between particularity and universality. Post-media, therefore, entails both equivalence – convergence made possible by shared standards – and its deployment in the production of singularities.

In his extended introduction, 'The Promise of Post-Media', Gary Genosko reminds us of Lyotard's observation that the term 'postmodernism' smacks of the modernist notion of a succession of cultural stages, and not the break with cultural linearity that postmodernism and post-media propose. And as Genosko explains, progress is never assured in the passage from one stage of socio-technical development to another. To have passed out of the mass media age by no means implies that we have left behind all its techniques of manufacturing mass conformity and normalisation. The relative user-unfriendliness of the early web guaranteed a plurality of forms which have long since evaporated in the development of a seamlessly slick Web 2.0. Net artists Olia Lianlina and Dragan Espenschied have recently resurrected the pages of Geocities in their *Digital Folklore* project to show how startlingly random and messy vernacular design on the web once was. The many-to-many medium found its aesthetic equivalent in a manifold of idiosyncratic styles. Recent web design and standards close down that expressive potential by offering a designed solution for everything, not least art production. This cleansing of the web space belies a darkening of its background activities: an asymmetrical landscape of surveillance, cyberwar, cybercrime, escalating energy consumption and the retailing of attention.

Post-media then, cannot simply be equated with the digital convergence and networking of media: it remains instead a tactics of singularisation and subjectification immanent to capitalism's programmatic conversion of all technologies into conduits of conformity. In light of this insight and in an attempt to extend the ramifications of post-media beyond the simply digital or technological realm, Cadence Kinsey insists, 'the question of post-media is pertinent not just in relation to recent artistic practices that engage with digital technology, but also, crucially, the histories and theories of modernism and conceptualism.' Drawing on the work of Rosalind Krauss in her late work on the conceptual artist, film-maker and poet, Marcel Broodthaers, Kinsey combines the art historian's notion of 'post-medium' with that of 'post-media'. Krauss herself asserts the necessarily 'plural' status of any medium at the end of the 20th century, the final death blow to certain modernist critics invested in 'thinking of an aesthetic medium as nothing more than an unworked physical support'.

It is out of this heteronomy that critical forms of autonomy associated with minor and micropolitical media wrest themselves. But it is also the convergence of media, their compatibility and articulation within emergent 'new' technologies, that creates the precondition for post-media positions and practices. Thus mass-media is far from completely eclipsed – a development not necessarily predicted by Guattari's vision of the next century. Instead we live under a condition in which top down communications from corporate actors and singular and particular enunciations from below travel and find their audiences via the same medium but along different channels. For Clemens Apprich this situation is the legacy of 'a constant interrelation between avant-garde experimentation and mass distribution' throughout the long 20th century. Guattari's perspective of post-media provides a fertile analysis of this relation precisely because it puts power relations to the fore of understandings of media. Rather than simply seeing their arrangement as symbolic of power, however, technologies become integral to the working out and struggles for its minor and molar forms. It is a condition which has increasingly been laid bare in the wave of revolts across Europe, the US, Latin America and the Middle East as the different means and forms of enacting power on the street are overlaid on the different means and forms of enacting power through media. As these feedback upon each other they disturb, interrupt and overflow respective modes of address and forms of engagement.

THE PROMISE OF POST-MEDIA

GARY GENOSKO

The doors for entrance and exit are not the same.
– Félix Guattari

Jean-François Lyotard once reminded us that the prefix post-, for which he was well known from his path-breaking report, *The Postmodern Condition*, in suggesting both a 'simple succession' and a 'new direction', remained 'perfectly modern'.[1] In this light any turn to post-media must recognise that the break from the mass into a new condition carries forward a good deal of baggage: instead of surpassing the past, elements of it are repeated. The break is not really clean and Lyotard has recourse to psychoanalysis to understand how his post- initiates an 'initial forgetting' that the modern is working through.[2] We know that Guattari, who identified the model of the psychoanalytic unconscious as even more reductionistic than the figures of subjectification generated on television, would develop schizoanalysis as a metamodel – a critique of models (norms, mediators, and patterns) and the 'submission to modern systems of alienation and "soft" exploitation.'[3] He would countenance no easy recourse to orthodox versions of psychoanalysis. For Guattari, however, the shift from mass into post-media would not be sequential and definitive but coexistent, contestatory, and messy. Indeed, a hallmark of Guattari's thought is the refusal of phasal developmental schemas and an insistence on simultaneous elaboration and a co-mingling polyphony. And Guattari vigorously protected his post- from association with postmodernism in order to avoid any suggestion that it might be apolitical and revolve around 'the paradigm of every submission and compromise with the existing status quo.'[4]

Writing in the late 1980s and early 1990s on the post-media hypothesis in a popular vein with a series of articles in *Le Monde* as well in the pages of the journal he co-founded with Gilles Deleuze, *Chimères*, Guattari speculated about entering into an era understood as post-mass in the sense that infotech interactivity would provide tools for resingularising otherwise passive and alienated audiences.[5] Guattari's withering criticism of capitalist mass mediatic subjectification as productive of a 'somnolent' population is directed at a transformative process that turns 'producer-consumer [prosumer] citizenry into serialized and desingularized, unoriginal zombies.'[6]

The rise of minoritarian user groups that he witnessed on the French videotex system connected through the national telephone network, Minitel, with new modes of organisation and the formation of new alliances around services, inspired Guattari to tentatively theorise a proto-internet as a site of desire driven by dissensus yet composing a collective diagram of commonalities. He was not so much concerned with the state telecommunications monopoly of France Télécom over Minitel, and the protectionism that defined this closed network. Rather, Guattari's focus was on a machinic subjectivity production that would undoubtedly change with political and technological developments (selling off state assets like the telephone system and the emergence of a more open and flexible internet), but which still gave rise to user-generated content and collective assemblages that promised a degree of self-management, even before the removal of the typical molar blockages such as the need to register and receive permission from the national telephone provider to offer a service.

Guattari sought enunciative singularity from his media, and if he could find it with a keyboard and screen, together with a few like-minded people, then this passion of a subject-group would suffice as an entry point into the post-mediatic age. He was well aware that technological evolution can both enhance and diminish processes of subjectification. Nothing progressive is guaranteed in the assemblage of the human and technological. He often mentioned zapping – channel surfing – as an ambivalent example of a collective refrain of affluent sleepwalkers, but also an instance of a more engaged audience, one with more choices (content, programming, scheduling) to be sure.[7] Much of the material that Guattari discussed as post-media was not overtly technological and concerned how the question of subjectification could be worked out against the tendency of capitalism to produce restricted versions of this process. In other words, Guattari sought out opportunities for 'new emancipatory social practices and above all alternative assemblages of subjective production' against capitalist tendencies to destroy collective values and recompose models of individualism and success.[8] Overcoming fatalism and conservatism required the formulation and pursuit of 'non-capitalist goals' that could not be hijacked by tired left-right political schisms.[9]

Reaching the post-media era is a programmatic goal of social ecology. Circa 1990, it looked like the potential media ecology would display a convergence of media – a networking, he muses of computer, telematic and television screens – with the important question being the capacity of creative users to utilise these systems in new ways due to a lowering of costs, widespread availability and portability through miniaturisation. Not at all referring to the NASDAQ, Guattari wondered: 'The information and telematic revolutions are supporting new "stock exchanges" of value and new collective debate, providing opportunities for the most individual, most singular and most dissensual enterprises.'[10]

Guattari's post- marks out transitions: from consensual mass to a dissensual post-mass media. Both Guattari and Lyotard were critical of consensus as a master narrative of the project of modern emancipation, and the subsequent abandonment of universals (models, orthodoxies) and grand narratives in both of their philosophies opens the way for localised survivals of these concepts, as opposed to a complete surpassing of them. Guattari was especially sensitive to the ways in which dissensus could be simulated for short-sighted gains, yet, in its most authentic forms, was worth fighting for as a fundamental right to non-equivalent self-engenderings in relation to other singular alterities, whose proliferation and the manners in which they are assembled cannot be reduced to human individuals or persons, trapped in binary schisms, or devastated by the profit motive.

Guattari defined Integrated World Capitalism (IWC) in terms of a description of global and post-industrial capitalism in which three evaluative terms are used: processes of machinic *production*; dominant economic-semiotic systems, considered in terms of the *market*; structures of social segmentation, considered in terms of the *state*. This mode of capitalist valorisation is described on the basis of the order of priority given to the three terms, in this case, production-market-state. The key features are that production is increasingly decentred and focussed on signs, and subjectivity, and that the capacity to integrate and exploit social diversity is unprecedented. Information and fluidity play key roles in this post-industrial capitalism that is marked threefold by modes of info-machinic production and a condition of permanent crisis; the market becomes transnational; and the state becomes minimal and speculative. In concert with these developments, mass media encourages cynicism and the abdication of political and ethical responsibility (postmodern abandon), and produces a subject reductionistically bound to equivalence and beholden to market fluxes.

By contrast, a new participatory post-media held great potential. Guattari believed that despite the work of the infantilising effects of mass media that survive into the post-media era, as he experienced in the broadcasting of the first Gulf War, the mass mediatic 'snare of Western subjectivity' could be reappropriated and resingularised.[11] Let's not forget that the urgency of shifting into a post-media era was underlined for Guattari during his viewing of the Gulf War on television. But it also concerned him greatly since he was worried about analphabeticisation (the effects of post-literacy such as short attentions spans and short-term memory and ephemerality) and the difficult to crack equivalence between media expression and the absence (masking and excluding) of singularity, a genuine incomparability so often subsumed by personalisation services that accessorise preformed identities. Post-media signifies resistance to these factors and the active 'aesthetic reappropriation of the production of images, and of audiovisual production', and becoming heterogeneous of homogenetic subjectifications.[12]

Given the saturation of Minitel in France, internet use circa 1990 remained very low and was slow to develop, hypertext was brand new, and the World Wide Web would not emerge until the following year, followed by the browsers that defined the early Web experience. Guattari's observations were understandably tentative because he did not live to see the promising new modalities of subjectification in action available in the World Wide Web. He didn't really talk about the Web, instead thinking in terms of planetary computerisation. Still, he did mention the promises of 'various "hypertexts"' to open up new means of connectivity, but circa 1991 these were still the purview of specialist technicians and not yet available to the artists, teachers and small subject-groups who could really utilise them. Guattari thought that hypertext might initiate a new form of writing more powerful than the Gutenberg revolution.[13]

In a post-mass media era the quality of interactions between users and creators shows potential to reinvent communication, redemocratise consumption, and enrich processes of subjectification in the pursuit of self-reliance. The Guattarian subject is produced and punctuated by points of singularity and transformed by exploring the potential consistencies they bear in the process of inventing autonomy. Subjectification is influenced by affects that stick to it and by refrains that count it out, both helping to build a territory in which it may existentially instantiate itself. Ecosophy contributes new incarnations inspired by artistic production. Famously, Guattari wrote that 'one creates new modalities of subjectivity in the same way that an artist creates new forms from the palette.'[14] When this palette is not longer paint but graphics programs, when access to computer-aided drafting/design is widespread, and the democratisation of special effects software has occurred, Guattari hoped that a new social ecology among producers, consumers, students, and teachers would emerge. He believed that it was not new combinations along the existing axis of private-public that would bring about change, because 'creation is wedged like a crowbar between public and private, neither of which assures its true freedom', rather, it would require novel configurations of production – what we see today in crowdsourcing and peer-to-peer networking.

Irreducible to a single common denominator, hence polyphonic, and indescribable in fixed genetic stages, subjectivity production is collective (and machinic) and self-posits through enunciative assemblages. Advances that provide new collaborative as opposed to proprietary platforms for assisting in the development of processes that are more complex, sustaining and enriching for subjectification, would in turn help to push media evoution in a more promising direction. 'We cannot expect positive repercussions from new technologies unless these technologies are adopted by way of individual and collective creative practices', Guattari maintained.[15]

Guattari's characteristically broad strokes were much in evidence when pointing a hopeful way forward. Guattari envisaged that limits on intellectual property would follow as more and more user communities got involved in infotechnology system design. Certainly, free and open-source software hackers have blazed important trails in inverting copyright with General Public Licenses.[16] In keeping with this theme, Guattari speculated about how research results should be shared, and 'industrial secrets' must be limited.[17] The struggles over trademarking genetic data are a case in point. He also believed that national media ethics commissions and public re-education programs would be founded to meet the challenges of corporate and state abuses of broadcast news media, especially in light of the first Gulf War's circulation of a dominant mass mediatic homogenesis of subjectification (the more one watches, the less one understands, and the more likely it is that one supports the action). These comments indicate that the transition from mass to post-media was stalling, and he called for 'an entire public (e)education program' about how news is presented, about who owns the networks, and the ways news may be democratised. Guattari did not mention citizen journalism, nor did he experience the emergence of one of the key figures of our time, whistleblowing websites and blogs.[18]

Guattari also sensed that media interconnectivity could have positive effects by developing new collective sensibilities. Guattari intuited that this would lead to minoritarian becomings linking local and regional upheavals to planetary problematics, suggesting the ways in which Web activism would come to cross constituences and organise on-and off-line actions. Post-media invokes a minor art precipitating non-countable, revolutionary becomings, freeing molecular components for new constellations – autonomous media like Insu'tv in Naples.

Guattari still believed in the future:

> The post-mediatic revolution to come will have to be guided to an unprecedented degree by those minority groups which are still the only ones to have realized the mortal risk for humanity of questions such as: the nuclear arms race; world famine; irreversible ecological degradation; mass-mediatic pollution of collective subjectivities.[19]

Guattari had already learned in the 1980s how the free radio movement in France made extensive use of Minitel services to constitute groups of supporters and this cross-platform minoritarian resistance was one of his primary points of reference for post-media. This is perhaps why, as a supporter of free radios in France, he did not strongly criticise Minitel on the basis of its statist and centralised status. Indeed, he understood the potential of the user groups on Minitel as akin to the offline transdisciplinary groups he created and moved in. These minoritarian assemblages were the incubators for post-media subjectifications, as they plotted paths between the sirens of IWC and state cooptation. What really impressed him was the the extent to which 'the promoters of these devices [like Minitel] had not foreseen the "indirect" uses which were to be made of them.'[20]

Dents in Guattari's optimism were evident, and he wavered in his enthusiasm about post-media:

> one is forced to admit that there are very few objective indications of a shift away from oppressive mass-mediatic modernity toward some kind of more liberating post-media era in which subjective assemblages of self-reference might come into their own.[21]

Franco Berardi has helpfully suggested that the Free Radio experiments of the 1970s in Italy and during the '80s in France in which both he and Guattari were involved were 'a general rehearsal' for the subversive resingularisations and destructuring of mass media that the web helped to bring to fruition.[22] As Guattari explained:

> But the point the organizers of the popular free radio stations particularly emphasize is that the totality of technical and human means available must permit the establishment of a veritable feedback system between the auditors and the broadcast team: whether through direct intervention by phone, though opening 'studio doors', through interviews or programs based on listener-made cassettes, etc. [...] We realize here that radio constitutes but one central element of a whole range of communication means [...].[23]

Guattari understood how Radio Alice kept sympathetic Bolognese informed about the riots in March 1977 by receiving reports by telephone and broadcasting them, but did not reduce this to a technical accomplishment. A free radio station is a node in a complex media ecology that is sustained by a micropolitics built upon experimentation that perfuses a social assemblage. Together Guattari and Berardi understood the power of the free radio movement as 'the first experiment of deterritorialisation of the telecommunications system' and as a catalyst for social change beyond the technical level in critiques of restrictive legislation, intellectual property, autonomy from traditional organisations, from all levels of government, etc.[24] For Guattari 'free radio is like a kind of match that you strike and then everything catches fire.'[25]

The molecular revolution might not be televised, but it would be tweeted. Social media relayed reports on the protests in Tahrir Square in Cairo during January and February of 2011 and had originally provided tools for the April 6 Movement.[26] Wireless connectivity was attacked by the state, and the highly centralised and totalitarian internet 'kill-switch' implemented. From a Guattarian perspective the parallels between free radio and social media are obvious at the technical level, and in both cases the violence of the state can be exercised to shut down but not silence post-mediatic tendencies towards resingularisation. Two years later protests against the government continue in Egypt. The typical reading of the role of social media by the mass media today is that they continue to play roles in disseminating information about activities as they unfold. But this in itself betrays the forward-looking example of free radios. When social media are simply reinscribed as 'instruments of information' they are remodelled as mass media, and the struggle for autonomy carried by multiple communications technologies, new social relations, and new sensibilities is diminished by the transmission function.[27]

Only rarely would Guattari remark on the dangers of control, modulation and surveillance within post-media; Big Brother was not the preordained outcome of new information technologies. He was certainly cognisant of these issues, but did not fully connect them with the exploitation of user data that we see today with the corporate internet and with threats to privacy (a notion that uncritically presupposes a preformed subject). He did not witness the Americanisation of global internet governance. He believed that singular productions of subjectivity that reappropriated media would be in some measure resistant to capitalistic exploitation, that is, not easily recuperable. His hopes for the passage into the post-media were tentative, acknowledging risk, warning about the fallout from violent deterritorialisations in the social field, and the ambivalent promises of new technologies bubbling up on the machinic phylum. Yet he mentioned that compact disks (rewritable media in general), cell phones, satellite television, television tuner cards for PCs, access to new databases – indeed, many then new 'technological mutations' could be used to enhance 'personal programming.'[28]

In Guattari's explanation of free radio experiments, he experienced most intensely how the semiotic polyvocity of speech returned to prominence through a machinic orality entailed by the daily mental ecological need for poetry (both written and performed) that nurtures processes of subjectification. On Radio Alice and Radio Tomate one could speak with one's mouth full; many people spoke at the same time, and this created new means of expression, and listening. This inspired Guattari to emphasise enunciative polyvocality. Free radio experimentation is indexed to the passage into the post-media era through heterogeneous machinic means like synthesized speech, promoting the creation of new and different enunciative assemblages, especially a focus on orality:

> The era of the digital keyboard will soon be over; it is through speech that dialogue with machines will be initiated.[29]

Guattari was inspired by spoken word and sound performance, Rap music, concrete poetry, and visits to the Polyphonix festivals (with friends Jean-Jacques Lebel and Sarenco). The text-heavy bulletin boards of the early web communities, as well as the low or no-graphics of teleputing which Guattari experienced, required more complex refrains built from musical aspects of speech. But neither were they like the pseudo-neutral voices of news readers nor the booming voices of super-ego leaders. Guattari imagined the future through the establishment of new conventions involving voice-machine enunciative assemblages, what we now call mobile communications with voice-command and recognition applications – though, even now, this is still an underdeveloped area.

But one of the most challenging dimensions of the post-media era is that critical attention will need to turn to machinic subjugation (an integrated piece 'enslaved by') rather than social subjection (an exterior piece 'subject to' a higher power).[30] A troubling consequence of the growing mutual imbrication of machines and processes of subjectification are networked interactions that actually minimise processes of subjectification. Thus, a machinic enunciation may take place as a result of the displacement of the anthropocentric perspective and with a sense that is strictly operational. I have elsewhere made the argument that the debit card and bank machine remain our best examples of this process, and Maurizio Lazzarato has described how credit cards make their users ('dividuals') into tributaries of the credit-machine, authentication and verification system.[31]

In an interview with Guattari undertaken only two months before his death, he stated what is perhaps the most perilous feature of post-media life. Eschewing surveillance, and keeping his distance from the genealogical opposition between regimes – societies of discipline developed by Foucault and societies of control suggested by Deleuze – Guattari applied his principle of coexistence to both forms of subjective integration, noting that control affirms a subjective modelisation based on the actions and obedience of 'a social robot', in other words, a strong machinic subjugation. He adds this remark: 'There isn't even any need to keep the subject under surveillance or control.'[32] Machinic subjugation to television was a real danger, and Guattari, in the depths of his own depression, could be found slumped in front of the tube. He understood the effects of serving as a tributary of the program, inhabiting an existential territory defined by the speaker (i.e., the talking head), hypnotised by the blue glow and cut off from his friends: enslaved like a robot, merely a flickering intersection of a televisual microassemblage. But it wasn't only television that posed a danger; playing video games or getting hung up on comic books were just as likely to constitute a circuit for the exchange of instructions. Subjugation catapults the user to the status of an integrated, intrinsic, component part. Feeding data into Google's constant refinements of its page rank algorithms with every initiated search is a more contemporary way of framing machinic enslavement in the digiverse. But even here the robotic character of inputted choice is not really adequately expressed. The diminishment of subjectification occurs within a field of so-called decisions about choices generated in advance on the basis of extrapolations from aggregated prior choices. The horizon is to apply past choices about the kind of objects selected and terms and images searched for without any further searching in full anticipation of any future decisions. The uncanniness of approximate experiences of this sort on websites like Amazon through its 'recommendations' is often humorous, but occassionally the results are eerily accurate when it comes to predicting, through automated analyses, personal preferences. This is a particularly fruitful direction for those interested in Guattari's post-media hypothesis.[33]

Infocapital's capacity to provide pseudo-singularisation is constantly enhancing itself and such a molar form of containment has inspired molecular constructions of resistance through the critical analysis of affective contagion, diagrams of distributed networks, and the internet of things. How does one hack a 'social robot'?

Finally, cycling back to the insight that what is meant by post-media must coexist with mass media forms reminds us that even the capacity to think through changes in media studies, for instance, the transition from network television to the post-network era, can be neither separated from the kinds of subjectification that viewer control, choice and non-linear viewing provide, nor from the circulation of affects, intersecting communications, complex refrains and ruptures of singularity (liberation) that help to complexify post-mediatic subjectifications.[34]

Footnotes

1   Jean-François Lyotard, *The Postmodern Condition*, Geoff Bennington and Brian Massumi (trans.), Minneapolis: University of Minnesota Press, 1984. Jean-François Lyotard, 'Note on the Meaning of "Post-"', in *The Postmodern Explained*, Julian Pefanis and Morgan Thomas (trans.), Minneapolis: University of Minnesota Press, p.76.

2   Ibid., p.80.

3   Félix Guattari, *Cartographies Schizoanalytiques*, Paris: Galilée, 1989, p.65.

4   Ibid., p.56.

5   The primary articles in this series are: 'La révolution moléculaire', *Le Monde* 7 December 1990; 'Pour une éthique des médias', *Le Monde* 6 November 1991 Translated as 'Toward an Ethics of the Media', (trans.) Janell Watson, *Polygraph* 14, 2002, pp.17–22; 'Ecologie et politique: Un nouvel axe progressiste', *Le Monde* 4 June 1992; and 'Vers une ère post-média,' *Chimères* 28 (printemps–été 1992). http://www.revue-chimeres.fr/drupal_chimeres/files/termin51.pdf 'Towards a Post-Media Era', (trans.) Alya Sebti and Clemens Apprich, in this volume pp.26.

6   Félix Guattari, 'Un nouvel axe progressiste', *Le Monde* 4 June 1992.

7   Félix Guattari, 'La révolution moléculaire', *Le Monde* 7 December 1990.

8   Félix Guattari, *Cartographies Schizoanalytiques*, op. cit., p.55.

9   Félix Guattari, *The Three Ecologies*, I. Pindar and P. Sutton (trans.), London: Athlone Press, 2000, p.62.

10 Félix Guattari, ibid., p.65.

11 Félix Guattari, 'Did You See the War?' in *Soft Subversions*, A. Loselle (trans.), New York: Semiottext(e), 1996, p.133.

12 Ibid., p.134.

13 Félix Guattari, 'Towards an Ethics of the Media', op. cit., p.19.

14 Félix Guattari, *Chaosmosis*, P. Bains and J. Pefanis (trans.), Indianapolis: Indiana University Press, 1995, p.7.

15   Félix Guattari,'Towards an Ethics of the Media', op. cit., p.19.

16   See Gabriella Coleman, *Coding Freedom: The Ethics and Aesthetics of Hacking*,
     Princeton: Princeton University Press, 2012, pp.69–70.

17   'Towards an Ethics of the Media', op. cit., p.20.

18   Ibid., p.20.

19   *Cartographies Schizoanalytiques*, op. cit., p.61.

20   'Towards an Ethics of the Media', op. cit., p.19.

21   Gary Genosko (ed.), *The Guattari Reader*, Oxford: Blackwell, 1996, p.98.

22   Franco Berardi, *Félix Guattari: Thought, Friednship, and Visionary Cartography*, C.
     Stivale and G. Mecchia (trans.), London: Palgrave Macmillan, 2008, p.31.

23   Félix Guattari, 'Popular Free Radio', (trans. D.L. Sweet), in *Soft Subversions*, op. cit.,
     pp.74–5.

24   Franco Berardi, *Félix Guattari*, op. cit., p.31.

25   Félix Guattari, *Molecular Revolution in Brazil*, K. Clapshow and B. Holmes (trans.),
     Los Angeles: Semiotext(e), 2008, p.171.

26   See, http://en.wikipedia.org/wiki/April_6_Youth_Movement

27   Franco Berardi, *Félix Guattari*, op. cit., p.31.

28   'Towards an Ethics of the Media', op. cit., p.18.

29   *Chaosmosis*, op. cit., p.97.

30   Gilles Deleuze and Félix Guattari, *A Thousand Plateaus*, Brian. Massumi (trans.),
     Minneapolis: University of Minnesota Press, 1987, pp.456–7

31   Gary Genosko, 'Guattari's Contributions to the Theory of Semiocapitalism', in *The
     Guattari Effect*, E. Alliez and A. Goffey (eds.), London: Continuum, 2011, pp.115–33
     and Maurizio Lazzarato, *The Making of the Indebted Man*, J.D. Jordan (trans.), Los
     Angeles: Semiotext(e), 2012, pp.148–9.

32   Félix Guattari, 'The Vertigo of Immanence: Interview with John Johnston', Andrew
     Goffey (trans.), in *The Guattari Effect*, op. cit., p.27.

33   I am indebted to the work of Neal Thomas for his Guattarian reflections on Google
     algorithms on his web site http://hivemedia.ca.

34   The idea of post-network theory has been developed by Amanda Lotz, *The Television
     Will Be Revolutionized*, New York: New York Univeristy press, 2007. I would like to
     thank my colleague Tanner Mirrless for bringing this work to my attention.

TOWARDS
A POST-MEDIA ERA

FÉLIX GUATTARI

Translated by Alya Sebti and Clemens Apprich,
with additional modifications by Neinsager

The junction of television, telematics and informatics is taking place before our eyes, and will be completed within the decade to come.

The digitisation of the television image will soon reach the point where the television screen is at the same time that of the computer and the telematic receiver. Practices that are separated today will find their articulation. And what are passive attitudes today may perhaps begin to evolve. Cabling and the satellite will allow us to zap through 50 channels, while telematics will give us access to countless image databases and cognitive data. The element of suggestion, even hypnotism, in the present relation to television will vanish. From that moment on, we can hope for a transformation of mass-media power that will overcome contemporary subjectivity, and for the beginning of a post-media era of collective-individual reappropriation and an interactive use of machines of information, communication, intelligence, art and culture.

Through this transformation the classical triangulation – the expressive chain [*chaînon expressif*], the object of reference [*l'objet référé*] and the meaning [*signification*] – will be reshaped. For instance, the electronic photo is no longer the expression of a univocal referent but the production of a reality among others. The television news was already composed of several heterogeneous elements: the figurability of the sequence, the modelling of subjectivity according to prevailing patterns, normalising political pressure, the concern to keep singularising ruptures to a minimum. At present such production of immaterial reality takes precedence in all fields, ahead of the production of physical connections and services.

Should one be nostalgic about 'the good old days' when things were as they were, regardless of their mode of representation? But did these 'good old days' ever exist anywhere other than in the scientific and positivist imaginary? Already, during the Paleolithic age – with its own myths and rituals – expressive mediation had distanced itself from 'reality'. In any case, all prior formations of power and their particular ways of shaping the world have been deterritorialised. Money, identity, social control fall under the aegis of the smart card. Far from being a return to earth, the events in Iraq made us lift off into an almost delirious universe of mass-media subjectivity. New technologies foster efficiency and madness in the same flow. The growing power of software engineering does not necessarily lead to the power of Big Brother. In fact it is way more cracked than it seems. It can blow up like a windshield under the impact of molecular alternative practices.

POST-MEDIA OPERATORS: 'SOVEREIGN & VAGUE'

HOWARD SLATER

First published in *Datacide* 7, August 2000[1]

No one recognises these powers as their own
 – Guy Debord

Why Theory?

We have to dispense with the idea that theorising occurs after the creative
event; that a poem or a track or a text is made and then, as part of its process
of dissemination, there follows the theorising of the piece. Such a theorising
is normally attributed to those known variously as critics, reviewers and
essayists. However, what actually occurs is that theorising goes on at the
same time as the creative event is being worked upon. It is complementary
to the event and, more importantly, it is the continuous precondition for
the event. There is always this theoretical supplement to any activity: a
carpenter fits cupboards into an alcove and there is this ongoing process
about the nature of the material, a questioning of the next step, and how
it is best to overcome those obstacles, such as the unevenness of the wall,
that present themselves. Similarly, when producers make a track there is a
similar theorisation going on: what sounds to use, how they fit in to other
sounds, how they relate to expectation, how best to structure the track. Such
a theoretical component to any activity is denied because theory is normally
attributed to a textual product, and like the role of the critic, this comes to
exercise the effect upon creative producers that their activity is somehow
'below' the level of theoretical process.

This self-deprecation, actively instituted by the division of labour (a
compartmentalisation of tasks that undoubtedly limits perception), serves
to reinforce the divide between consciousness and activity, between thought
and action; it severs the creative producer from the consciousness of his
or her activity to the point that the theoretical component is occluded.
However, if there wasn't an 'auto-theoretical' element to activity, which
always includes context and reciprocity and which, if made conscious, can
defy the division of labour and its instating of various dualities such as that
between perception and conception, then there could be no next creative
event as the process of engagement is always giving rise to tangents and
possible ideas for the next poem, text or track. There is a thinking and an
engaging with materials at the same time. Praxis. Process. Bearings that, in
the slipstream of the creative event, offer an inkling of objectives, limitations

and, crucially, autonomy. Process premisses change. To deny this ever-present and constant theoretical activity, these re-orientations that include memory, endless self-interpretation and renewed possibility, is to conform to a definition of theory that is imposed: 'it is forgotten that experience can inform theory, that theory is in itself a form of experience, that there is such a thing as a theoretical practice.'[2]

Perhaps a theorising that neglects such auto-theoretical aspects could be termed 'discourse' and that this latter form of theoretical activity is so often hermetic, self-referencing and exclusionary is maybe because it seeks to resolve problems 'once-and-for-all' within a text rather than filtering these through an activity that is constantly posing these problems anew as a part of daily practice. In this way, by corralling theory into servicing their own renewal, academics do not confront the division of labour (the provisos of their knowledge) and instead reproduce the hierarchisation that not only occludes but occults the shared auto-theoretical component. Such hermetic academic discursivity – seen in the proliferation of secondary texts that veil and seek to possess the primary text – serves as a means of formalising the 'right' to theory; specialising it as a work of discipline that is divorced from 'practical energies'. Yet, to re-create what is meant by 'theorising', to refuse to differentiate it from 'everyday' activity, experience and experiment is to be engaged in a process of de-conditioning; a translating and de-translating of the 'inexhaustible stores of material' that, by means of memory and conscience, make of everyone an auto-theorist. Such a process, in not confining problems to discourse nor in seeking to compress them within formal, dispassionate and conclusive restraints, is a process of social engagement. Not knowing of boundaries, not even knowing of taught techniques of cross-over, the *sui generis* sites of communication proliferate and as they do it becomes clearer that, beyond the models offered by the media and the academy, it becomes a matter of re-appropriating the means of written, visual and aural expression. This approach is, in part, what those conspicuous outsiders, the situationists, meant by 'drifting': a reflective activity is not solely a matter of a 'large table and piles of books' but is as much a matter of the social-interaction of 'walking': a non-discursive sense of the environment.[3] This situationist take on auto-theorisation, which relates to the Marxist sense of critique as opposed to criticism, was partly employed to differentiate their activity from academia and, if, today, this auto-theoretical dimension has been supplanted by the discursive, making this dimension invisible to practitioners who self-deprecatingly deny its existence to themselves, it is sadly sought and reconvened in the pages and sites of the media where, not only does it fall to journalists to articulate our activity for us, it is, as a result of such voluntary delegation, a matter of creative producers searching for a 'scene' anywhere other than in their own auto-theoretical potential to be engaged.

Media Pimps?

However, such flight from the academic and discursive towards the 'free space' of the reputedly popular not only reveals the still 'clinging folds of the gown' (street cred as another form of seeking after acceptance), but it does hardly anything to resuscitate and encourage auto-theorisation. Disciplining structures are still operative. The exchange of one set of exigencies for another reveals that the choice between academia and the media (the false choice of rigour versus hedonism, earnestness versus noncommittalism) is one which posits, at best, an acute negotiation between dissemination and compromise and, at worst, a blind innocence bordering on unconscious collusion; an innocence that is in part an innocence of seeking after the legitimating word of arbiters but which is also a naivety undercut by an unsureness of motive – a lack of any other social context other than that of hermetic careerism (one slot becomes the advert for another slot). Yet the increasing merger of the academic and media markets (whose flagships currently seem to be post-rave culture studies, cybermania and 'brit-art') can be seen in their cancelling each other out in a neutralising blur of middle-ground and failed populsim (inner-sanctums and exclusivity still reign). Creativity, the free-flow of desire, becomes channelled into a playful and distracted entertainment but it is still a creativity that is eulogised with an overload of super-superlatives. And so, as with academic eulogies to creativity, when the mainstream media discusses creative processes it is normally couched in terms of what makes a poem, text or track 'better' than someone else's. That the 'Harvard System' of annotation is replaced by the interview situation does not diminish the degree of reverence. The canonical and the popular still resound to the familiar ring of 'genius', but in the media things are maybe worse in that a premature acclaim or interest in a creative producer can work to sap auto-theorisation by making the processes that inform the creativity into the motor of a production line: famous for a product, that product is replicated; famous for being misrepresented, the misrepresentation is promulgated. Often creative producers can almost be heard to be in the thrall of the mediatised situation

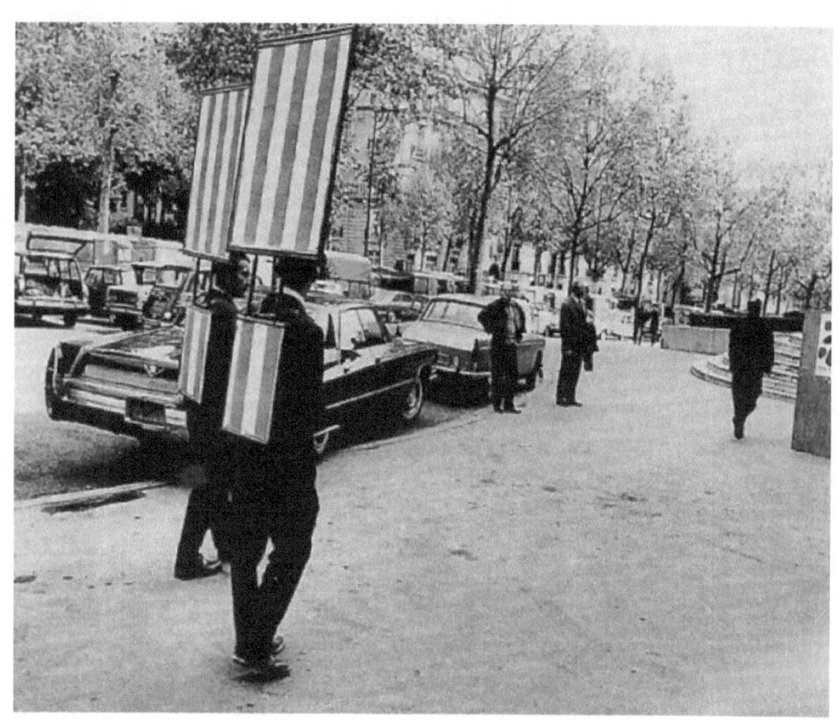

Daniel Buren, *Sandwich Men*, 1968, Paris

where, with the interviewer engaged in the dynamics of ego-activation, the interviewee is less likely to take the opportunity to talk in more general terms that could offer encouragement to others. If this does occur, if there is talk of social context and an interplay of engaged relations, if there is a straying from monadological specifics, then the journalistic editing process slips into action to select statements, re-write statements, or maybe even, if the contents of the discussion are too eclectic and tangential and hence veer towards the 'political', drop the feature altogether. The most successful manipulators of the media are those who know that they are dealing with the promotion of their own product (themselves) and, rather than pre-empt a critic's review and move out from the 'silent' confines of the interview situation, they choose, in many ways, to meet media censorship with self-censorship. This is the price of their pleasure: that their desire, which becomes ours, is a stopped-flow called entertainment.

But, crucially, one of the primary elements of auto-theorisation is the fact that it is dependent on being flawed and tentative. It is a space where mistakes and *meconnaissance* play a vital role. The media space is, however, by and large, one of celebration, one where 'success' and the finalisation of product are reified into something that is unchanging. It is at this point, when the creative producer is immersed in 'promotional time', that the media comes to exercise its seductive and parasitical prowess. The media has itself created this 'promotional time' and in conformity to it the creative producer comes to take time out, has a vacation in the media, so to speak, and discusses and pontificates on his latest book, album or exhibition. This media space requires that its subjects, obedient and pliable in the long sought after first-flush of acclaim, suspend their self-critical faculties to the point that enthusiasm can be wrought into the unadulterated jubilance of publicity (every opportunity to speak becomes a retrenchment). This celebratory context of promotion – self-censored and thus certain – can make most people who enter this framework come across as no less arrogant and self-contained than the discursive products of a scorned academy. However, if the latter have citations and references with which to instil an idea of collaboration the media has very little time for 'movements' or the tracing of nebulous and enigmatic social networks and, because not a few creative producers are in a state of 'denial' about the immediate influences of their peer group (scene), what is normally cited are the standardised historic reference points that best express the ambition of their particular situation (the right references). As all this creative activity is based on self-theorisation and is informed by the daily exchange of practice, concepts and techniques and as a means of testing these theories amidst those developed by the self-theorisation of others, it is this component that the media is quick to edit-out and it is aided in this by the creative producer who, even if he or she wants to, doesn't get the time to broach this aspect. The elementary social factor becomes off-limits. This media censorship of mistakes, its obfuscation of the frustrations of the auto-theorising process and its edited sacrifice of the collective aspect of creativity is what makes it function to deny the existence of struggle, uncertainty and collaboration: 'Origin in something else counts as an objection, as casting a doubt on value.'[4] For the media everything has to be unique and complete and its casting of the creative producer as 'the first' is achieved by denying the presence of precursors or allies. Instantaneity creates its own vacillating value and hyperbole raises the inflationary stakes until we've got a situation wherein the 'clued-up' servants of the media seem to be churning out the simulacra of hoaxes and pranks normally attributed to such cultural saboteurs as the KLF.

The media can't celebrate process or becoming. That would be to begin to suppress itself and, at the end of that fine day, it would be possible for us to return the creative product to its prosaic reality, bring it down from the reified air of its presupposed future posterity and install it as a social product. But in the meantime an air of unreality ensues. Everyone begins to expect a non-existent perfection and, awaiting their turn in the spotlight, are unable to address each other without the glare of this fictive mirror. Comparison, the bench mark of media quality control, equivalises value and starts to infect a scene which, abandoning its idiosyncratic drive, begins to compete and then, exhausted, reproduces the norm only to find it is too early or too late. For this divisive simulation to catch us in its thrall it is necessary for the 'invisible structures' of the media to remain unilluminated.

Journalistic construction is dependent on many elements, processes, that do not find their way into finalised articles or reviews. There is the selection of subjects, which elevates some at the expense of others (reinforcing hierarchy, individualism and competitiveness) and which is, more often than not, carried out in relation to readership expectation: a fictive, self-perpetuating and generalising factor, that itself continually passes through discussions with editors, sub-editors, circulation-managers and financiers. Perhaps at this stage there is consideration of factors such as the ease of access to subjects; the discussion of what is currently being supplied to pose as demand; the need for exclusivity, to be the first, to set trends. These are factors that establish a media mind-set where, above all, a kind of narcissistic investment in 'profession' is mistaken for objectivity:

the media not only 'constructs' the popular, as if the 'popular' pre-existed its journalistic mediation, but it then adheres to this definition of the 'popular' and thus perpetuates it. This mythic shading of the media would be quite interesting if it wasn't, as with all blind faith, so insidious, so in touch with the unconscious, so much a built 'drive' that modelises people. But as with 'heaven', access to the media is a fraught and self-immolating path. Not just anyone can get in, for access to the media becomes a slow trickle because introjection of the 'new' has to be couched in terms of the already pre-existing and discovery of the contemporaneous is overshadowed by the preparation of the 'new'! That there is a constant obedience to these exigencies of the profession via editors and that this obedience effects a journalist's modes of perception and communication means that even when research is carried out it cannot be turned into a 'processual' endeavour, a means of extending self-theorisation, but must be directed towards the final piece whose outcome is, before even being written, somehow already expected (its syntax and superlatives are already capitalistic). This relates to the journalistic trade in 'symbolic capital' where, in order to increase assignments (and assignments vary in prestige), there is a sense that whatever is said in an interview situation is subject to its being filtered via the journalist's own agenda: an agenda that may encompass... subservience to an editor to ensure the status of regular contributor... to the seeking-out of subjects and material that fits neatly into the tenor of a long-term approach (the thesis). In the latter instance the pay-off is that the journalist enters into an exchange with a creative practitioner whereby the latter is offered the promise of diffusion because the journalist is structurally placed as a gatekeeper permitting access to a means of mass distribution and potential popularity. This latter point is itself problematic for the unconscious dynamic which pervades such an exchange is one of censorship where the whole mythic idea of the popular (saved by visibility/ made subject) becomes a fear of being unpopular (dammed by invisibility/ made abject) and, like a child who seeks approval, we are witness to one means by which the media induces infantilism: there is a rush to conform to the proscribed limits of behaviour and thought, to seek not to be marked out, to never say or encourage anything politically contentious, to agree with that which flatters. But, there is another aspect of these journalistic 'invisible structures' that are left unspoken and edited-out: cronyism. Here a meeting between a creative producer and a journalist is one that is mutually complimentary rather than one that constitutes an interrogative opposition. Both know the score and both use each other. Like any professionalism, adaptation to such 'invisible structures' is an easily acquired virtue, because quite simply, conformity is dependent on the continuing acceptance of what is.[5] They are seen as 'virtues' because, in relying on the suspension of auto-theorising and adhering to the job specification, they are socially adaptive.

Media Whores?

Everyone knows a media whore when they see one. It's pointless making a list because most people have their own. They're the ones that crop up everywhere and at every available opportunity. It's not so much that they are acclaimed by many or that their persisting visibility is a mark of 'quality'. No. The media-whore is one on their own. One of a kind. A grafter in more ways than one. A grifter and a grafter. A convenient success symbol for the ongoing pliable acceptance of the non-guaranteed freelance culture of 'creative' self-exploitation. It is a question of professionalism meeting professionalism, of slotting into the requirements with all the smooth politeness of a parasite. Thus the media whore (one long disavowal) is trusted. Deadlines can be met. Appointments adhered to. Soundbites well rehearsed. There will be no time wasting. No arguments about context because the media whore is the context. A one-man band; a one-man context. So, not knowing the full extent of an activity the media whore springs to mind as the delegate of that activity and is endlessly invited to appear, perform and contribute by people hoping to attract enough of an audience to justify the grant. For the more the person-product is seen and reported, the more it becomes increasingly predictable, the more its repetition attracts the hip academics who come to view the output as having the necessary consistency to merit coverage in overviews. In this way the already mediatised is further mediated but this mediation doesn't stop because the media whore, being under contractual pressure to produce, will never complain about how s/he is to be represented because representation (the marketing of the 'self') is all that is wanted and the more prisms of representation (advertisements) there are to refract through then the more the hall of mirrors reflects, rather than distorts, the face of the media-whore. This is the instantaneity of the 'year zero of faciality' which Deleuze and Guattari vehemently speak out against:

> It is not the individuality of the face that counts but the efficacy of the ciphering it makes possible [...] This is an affair not of ideology but of economy and the

organisation of power [...] Certain assemblages of power require the production of a face.[6]

The media whore is a cipher that functions as an ever replenishing blank that only those who excel at mistaking obedience for desire can see; an equivalence blissfully unaware of context and motive; a cipher noted for the manufacture and delivery of goods; a conduit towards the building of an acculturating capitalism that proclaims equal but limited opportunities. This, then, is the 'circularity of circulation' in which the media-whore is caught: the same always proclaimed from a slightly different perspective (the tempered idiosyncrasy of a new journalist on the team), the same softened by academic attention (the researcher looking for thesis-matter). But it's a nice trap. For being visible attracts more visibility because visibility is not seen as the empty modus operandi of the media but as a mark of legitimation, a site, even, for the barely avowed projection of envy.

Recuperating the Media?

The episode of the media whore reveals one major facet of the media: its selection of subjects and its continual presentation of them allows people to be witness to the way that the media constructs the narrow dimensions of its ever expanding circle. What's more, if one of the functions of the media has been a kind of A&R, the elevation of certain subjects that are supposed to merit attention, then, in a post-media scene the effect is reversed. Here, the need to avoid being overloaded by options and choices comes to be filtered via the media in that the choices and options it offers are, on the whole, rejected. The media is used as a guide of what to avoid for, if a creative producer has untroubledly passed through the filter mechanisms of mediation, then it is probable that the product, sharing or overlapping with the media mind-set, the promotion of 'that which is', is similarly charged with the consensus inducing properties of the well adjusted (it has no traumatic qualities). But, a post-media attitude is not an anti-media attitude. We are begrudgingly attentive to the media because, living in a nuance of the same world, its effects cannot be escaped from and, more positively, it is through the media that capitalism articulates itself. The media, a negative injunction, instates the social with an updated set of contradictions that are always in the process of being played-out and if these processes are not highlighted by the media they can be covered and articulated in post-media contexts. Jean Baudrillard expresses a facet of this contradiction when he asks, 'Are the mass media on the side of power in the manipulation of the masses, or are they on the side of the masses in the liquidation of meaning, in the violence done to meaning?'[7] Baudrillard's playful question points to the question of subjective agency and whether this should speak for itself or have others speak for it; whether it should seize the media apparatus or rejoice in the 'devolution' of choice and responsibility. This points to contrasting political strategies that can, in a post-media context, exist side by side. There is the recognisably 'political' position of constituting ourselves as 'subjects, to liberate, to express ourselves at any price' and the position of the obstinate and truculent 'mass', the object at which the media messages are aimed and which involves 'the refusal of meaning and the refusal of speech [...] the hyperconformist simulation of the very mechanisms of the system, which is another form of refusal by overacceptance.'[8] Whereas Baudrillard is trying to refute the thesis that the 'mass' is manipulated by the media and that it requires 'enlightened' intellectuals to show it the way towards liberation, he is maybe, by adhering to the cumbersome and undifferentiated concept of 'mass', not going far enough in imbricating these two positions. The post-media operators, as those that function in a space-between 'media' and 'academy', do not identify as being either intellectual or mass, and being both authors and punters, composers and listeners, artists and spectators, their position, informed by the diffuse energies of desire, is constantly shifting. This is what makes it an autonomous practice and being one that is unrestricted by the paradigms of 'feature' and 'thesis' it can be free to articulate the findings of its own transversality. For instance, if an increase in information marks the present times and if this increase is producing 'uncertainty', a confusing array of choices and strategies, then this uncertainty can be recuperated by post-media operators to effect each pole of Baudrillard's playful dichotomy: we are no longer certain of being political subjects identified as working class or communist, but we are also no longer resting assured in our refusal to speak and answer back. We are no longer cadre or mass, 'contacts' or consumers, and this is where the auto-theorising component comes into it, for, as post-media operators, we are continually engaged in elucidating the nuances of context and situation and the theorising – in many ways a non-verbal theorising in that it includes gesture, image and sound – is propelled by the particular exigencies of varying situations (it is a resistance to legitimatising models in favour of a 'method' of desire; an opening up of micro-political dimensions; an instinctual transversalism). If we are always working class and militant then our reactions come to be predictable but, even so, we cannot allow this dimension to disappear completely, implying as it does a resistance to the monopoly of the means of distribution by means of becoming expressed by a misuse of the increasingly available means of production. Yet, if in a situation we remain silent our silence is read as a legitimating compliance and, yet, this same silence can maybe make a supposed quietude pregnant with obstinate incredulity whilst also allowing 'transference' to take place: the media, in the rush to say anything, reveals itself and draws our prognosis. This chameleon-like activity is maybe a post-media recuperation of journalistic practice but, unlike the bounded and professionally sanctioned dissimulation of journalists, we inadvertently merge Baudrillard's two strategies, and make theory and practice become co-incidental. This form of becoming, of never having remained, of being a 'lingering residuum', may in fact have been spurred on by the media's collusion with the constant overproduction of an acculturating capitalism, but a further post-media recuperation of it allows us to be dispersed rather than localisable, just as power is itself dispersed and not present in any one space or molecule. Beyond the pleasure principle lies auto-theorisation.

The media is recuperated at every turn. From the aping of a record review that imbues this promotional form with an intensity and a social meaning to the establishment of websites as nodes of research that are independent from the media and the academy, the post-media practice learns from 'the exteriority of its vicinity'.[9] Both connected to and autonomous from the media, it is like Marx's proletariat who, on the receiving end of the capitalist mode of production in the factories and workspaces, know instinctively the meaning of the methods that are employed on it: manipulation may be met with silence but it casts back a disgust at the barefacedness of the manipulator, a disgust that accumulates and, thus intensified, draws others into the orbit of conflict (in this case a conflict over the prevailing culture of compliance). Whereas a workforce, organised into unions, may too often have fought sectional battles, the creative producers of a post-media scene are disorganised to the extent that their sectional interests, becoming increasingly transversal, see points of contact and unification in their shared dismay of the inhibiting methods, form and content of the media.[10] So just as a vicinity to the media makes for an over-familiarisation that effects a withdrawal of interest and the establishment of alternative media spaces, the media's persisting misrepresentation of activity leads to the recuperation of misrepresentation as a device to manipulate the media. In all cases vicinity breeds a contempt that increases to the degree that, as with wage labour, a connectedness lays the grounds of an ever threatened disconnectedness.

Just as an increasing exposure to exploitation at the workplace provokes the development of means to subvert the contractual obligations of the workplace by means of petty theft, absenteeism, brewing-up, ridiculous union demands etc., so too are media messages recuperated by a choosing and filtering of messages: Throbbing Gristle used to recommend turning the sound of the TV down and playing music as its soundtrack but there are a myriad of other possible détournements that can range from consciously using the media's banalities as a way of 'switching-off' through to using it as a means to activate the energy of disgust. What occurs throughout is that the media's power is negotiated and post-media operators are, in a sense, manipulating their own manipulation; becoming conscious of the fact that social manipulation is instituted.[11] Not only does this reveal the role of the media in this manipulation – its homogeneity assured by the editorial diktat, the elevation of central signifiers and models of perception – it also brings into focus the receptive power of the post-media operators themselves; a power that, because it has diversified the levels at which it can place itself, achieves an imperviousness to a further conductance of those censorious and mediating powers of the media – it makes meaning doable. By means of the 'exteriority of its vicinity' it is empowered enough to be overpowered and, as a result, is sensitised to the dispersion of power which is not solely conducted through the channels of the media. Crucially, then, it comes to 'recognise these powers as its own' and, in so doing, the post-media operators, absconding from the quietism of the workplace, come to effect an expropriation of the means of expression.

Towards Self-Institution?

Auto-theorisation allows us to inhabit such contradictory spaces without having to synthesise them or choose between them. It is dependent on being flawed and tentative and relies upon mistakes as the tangential material of its own engagement; a material that places in relief the overproduced and hermetic products so feted by the media. Thus post-media activity is not the outcome of a discursive resolution, which would only lead to another discourse, but is the process that allows contradictions to be pushed in the direction of enigmas and provocative alloys. It allows for experimental positions without co-ordinates, it drifts off the map, flees from forced identification (and forced subjectivisation) and takes with it the masks and tools that would enslave it. And so, auto-theorisation is a constant vigilance, a controlled loss, a permutability of the rational and the unconscious. A processing of the self revealing social process. Being both screen and projector, receiver and sender, silent and voluble, being the margins of a centre that doesn't exist, it occupies a liminal position that, in continually being dispersed, coincides and overlaps with a post-media practice whose overall rhythms are broader (a breadth that can turn to history and precursors). Being a no-space, being illegitimate, means that the academy can be plundered and the media copied, but rather than ape these and look for a 'new' that fits into the criteria, post-media operations, by claiming back the auto-theoretical dimension, affirm those subjects and projects that are omitted: there is a place for history as opposed to nostalgia, for autobiography rather than biography, for militancy rather than quietism, for continuity rather than immediacy, for dirty timbre rather than slickness, for abnormal rather than normalising forms. The post-media operators, being attracted to process via auto-theorisation, are drawn to those cultural products that are conducive to propelling the process of discovery they are already engaged in. In brief these are products that are critical of consensus and which draw attention to the determining 'invisible structures': the selection and editing techniques that act to overcode and delimit the powers of reception; they are, to a certain degree, free of being over-encumbered by prior interpretation and in this way can function as sites for a 'practice of freedom': a freedom of thought, a freedom of language and a freedom of sound. Practices that could not be pursued through the media or the academy. This thumbnail description may sound reminiscent of the avant-garde, yet just as there is a definite coincidence, fuelled by a historical inquisitiveness denied them in the media, the post-media operators, not being aligned to the strictures of categorisation nor to the traps of visibility, would enter into the same relation to the avant-garde as it does the media: one of 'exterior vicinity'.

A common objection to post-media practice is that by not following the 'popular' route, by not conforming to an expectation of boundaries, it is not only difficult to locate but, in theorising its own paradigm, it is difficult to understand. Such accusations are themselves indicative of a desire to maintain the status quo for if a cultural product becomes too easily digestible, if it is too readily understood, then any thought of participating in the production of its meaning is left to those cognoscenti for whom meaning is a currency that defines what is. By accepting what is already present, by becoming overawed or enervated by it, we are closing down the possible areas where the 'social can be enacted', as it is the nuances of our own positions, their idiosyncrasies, that can, in creating meaning through combining meanings, be a spur towards action. This is precisely what the media denies. Its immediacy, the instantaneity of its communication, creates 'a climate hostile to action whose effect is only visible over time'.[12] Such generalised conditions of impatience that the media induces throughout society becomes translatable as a reluctance to take the time to understand and participate in anything. This in turn, in another turn of 'circular circulation', another conformity to the rhythms of the media, becomes the reason that familiar forms, familiar sounds and familiar language are always invoked. They save time, save us from the implications of our own 'doing', and, in providing the cushion of digestibility, come to form a bulwark against auto-theorisation. Thus it is maybe a case that we 'understand' too much and in 'understanding' we replicate what is when really what is absent, and what the post-media operators are intent on providing, is a sense of 'radical imagination', a transversal engagement, that is spurred on by using desire as the method: being free to go anywhere, free to draw on anything, free to say anything, unmoored and without vested interest is to, perhaps, after Castoriadis, to bring another mode of Being into existence, a Being that is self-instituting and is its own mode of 'self-alteration, its own temporality.'[13] Yet, whether this results in the institution of a 'new class' whose freedom is the freedom of working 'outside the sphere of material production proper'[14] or whether it is the opportunity for a social fiction entitled Post-Media Operators – Sovereign and Vague to be written, is, so the media have taught us, by the by; for it has been said now and said is as good as read and read is as good as real and, so the media have taught us, to write is to recuperate hype.

Footnotes

Title is drawn from two chapter headings in Adilkno's book 'Media Archive' Autonomedia,1998 // Text spurred on by Pierre Bordieu's 'On Television and the Media' Pluto,1998 // A version of this text (remixed by Jakob Jakobsen) appeared in *Infotainment* No.5.

1   http://datacide.c8.com/post-media-operators-%e2%80%9csovereign-vague%e2%80%9d/

2   Jean Laplanche, *New Foundations of Psychoanalysis*, Oxford/Cambridge, Mass.: Blackwell, 1989. Laplanche speaks of this ongoing theoretical activity as auto-theorisation: 'It is the inexhaustible stores of material that each human being in the course of existence strives to translate into his acts, his speech and the manner in

which he represents himself to himself [...] upon which the auto-theorisation of the human being seizes.'

3   Nietzsche, in retorting to Gustave Flaubert's contention that 'one can only think and write when sitting down', replies by saying 'only ideas won by walking have any value'.

4   Friedrich Nietzsche, *Twilight of the Idols*, Penguin, 1974.

5   Friedrich Nietzsche, 'What is, does not become; what becomes, is not... Now they all believe... in that which is.'

6   Gilles Deleuze and Félix Guattari, *A Thousand Plateaus: Capitalism and Schizophrenia*, Athlone, 1988.

7   Jean Baudrillard, 'The Masses' in *The Baudrillard Reader*, Blackwell, 1988.

8   Ibid.

9   Michel Foucault, *The Archaeology of Knowledge*, Routledge,1995.

10 Each 'scene' seems to be served by its 'own' media – music, art, cyberart, literature, film etc. – and whilst this isn't the place to go into this ghettoisation that results from the division of labour expressed in the form of specialisation it is worth pointing out that post-media is a practice that cuts across the nominal ghettos and rejects such categorical divisions of knowledge and vocabulary. Interestingly the renewed attention paid to the 'conceptual art' of the late '60s and early '70s can itself be seen as a spur towards a post-media awareness. The practice of artists like Kosuth, Baldessari, Buren, Latham, Art & Language, Metzger, etc. with their 'acceptance of the multiplicity of non-art subject matter' and being loosely cast as 'the de-materialisation of the art object' was indicative of an auto-theorising dimension that, with hindsight, can segue, not untroubledly, into that of the early Situationists, Alexander Trocchi's Project Sigma, Fluxus and Mail Art. Autonomous publishing was an important facet of all these groups and took in such activities as the production of journals as well as the making of conceptual artworks that were dependent on buying space in the media, making the catalogue the 'art', curator as artists, textual paintings etc. In movie land, the work of Godard (long despised as a Maoist) seem remarkably 'post-media' especially works like *One Plus One* and *Masculin/Feminin* with their use of sound and text and their transversal melding of poetry and polemic. (An article on Godard should appear in the next issue of *Datacide*).

11 In this way the post-media operators are maybe responding to Marx's request for the formation of a class which has radical chains, which does not want to redress a particular wrong but 'wrong in general' and which claims no 'traditional status but only a human status', i.e. a non-status, an equality. See Karl Marx, *Selected Writings*, T. Bottomore and M. Rubel (eds.), Pelican 1961, p.90.

12 Pierre Bordieu, *On Television and the Media*, Pluto,1998.

13 Cornelius Castoriadis, *The Imaginary Institution of Society*, Polity Press, 1987, p.372. See also: 'The time of doing must be instituted so as to contain singularities that are not determinable in advance, as the possibility of the appearing of what is irregular [...] it must preserve or make room for the emergence of otherness.'

14 Karl Marx, ibid, p259.

FÉLIX AND ALICE IN WONDERLAND: THE ENCOUNTER BETWEEN GUATTARI AND BERARDI AND THE POST-MEDIA ERA

MICHAEL GODDARD

The Enigma of the Post-Media Era

Towards the end of his life, Félix Guattari made several enigmatic suggestions about the emergence of a 'Post-Media era' that would have the effect of displacing or at least de-centring the hegemony of the mass media as we still know them today. Some of these references are extremely hermetic, for example the essay entitled 'Entering the Post-Media Era' tells us almost nothing about what would constitute it, except that it would be the result of a schizoanalytic, minority production of subjectivity whether on an individual, relational, group or micropolitical level leading to 'soft subversions and imperceptible revolutions that will eventually change the face of the world, making it happier.' The rest of the essay is devoted instead to an articulation of schizoanalysis along these lines. Elsewhere, in the essay 'Regimes, Pathways, Subjects', he referred to a third pathway/voice of subjective self-reference complementing those of power and knowledge (clearly referencing Foucault) and associated this path directly with the post-media era:

> Only if the third path/voice takes consistency in the direction of self-reference—carrying us form the consensual media era to the dissensual post-media era – will each be able to assume his or her processual potential and, perhaps, transform this planet - a living hell for over three quarters of its population - into a universe of creative enchantments.[1]

One might be tempted to interpret these enigmatic utopian statements with respect to subsequent developments of such interactive communicative technologies as the internet and their related social practices of network culture; after all Guattari's interest in the, then primitively developed, French Minitel system is well known. But, since Guattari was always less interested in new technologies per se than the collective assemblages of enunciation that they become the operators of, it is necessary to take a step back from any naïve assumption that what Guattari was engaging with was simply the coming culture of digital networks. Furthermore this technological essentialism is ruled out by Guattari himself, who earlier in the same essay poses this key question:

> Why have the immense processual potentials bought forth by the revolutions in information processing, telematics, robotics, office automation, biotechnology and so on, so far only led to a monstrous reinforcement of earlier systems of alienation,

an oppressive mass-media culture and an infantilising politics of consensus? What would make it possible for them to finally usher in a post-media era, to disconnect themselves from segregative capitalist values and to give free rein to the first stirrings, visible today, of a revolution in intelligence, sensitivity and creativity?[2]

This is not to say that Guattari's post-media era has nothing to do with network culture, whose development can certainly be seen to realise and confirm some aspects of the rhizomatic, machinic thought Guattari developed both alone and with Gilles Deleuze. Rather this link will be shown to be more complex and to pass via other fields of media experimentation and thought, especially that which emerged around 'popular free radio' in Italy in the 1970's and which was strongly associated with Guattari's friend Franco Berardi or 'Bifo'. The key element in any media or post-media assemblage is that of the production of subjectivity, which for Guattari is a directly political or micropolitical phenomenon and this is why the example of Italian free radio and Radio Alice was of such interest to him. To show the transversal relations between the theories and practices of Guattari and Berardi we will largely use as a map Berardi's own book, *Félix Guattari: Thought, Friendship and Visionary Cartography* which much more than a simple memorial or record of a friendship is a continuation of Guattari's rhizomatic thought that brings out very important and neglected aspects of Guattari's personal trajectory and work, precisely in relation to the question of an emergent post-media sensibility.[3] But before this it is worth examining the other side of this relation by means of some of the texts Guattari devoted to Italian media, or rather post-media, experiments such as Radio Alice which Berardi was directly involved with.

Millions and Millions of Alices in Power

In the late 1970s Guattari devoted several texts to the phenomenon of popular free radio and especially that taking place in Italy. 'Why Italy?' is the essay that gives the clearest indication of why he considered this such an important phenomenon.[4] First of all there is the concrete context: he has been asked to introduce the French edition of *Alice e il Diabolo*, the principle documentation of this radio and its political trajectory, which interests him since it is an explicitly situationist and Deleuzo-Guattarian radio constituting an auto-referential feedback loop between rhizomatic thought and media subversion. More importantly, Radio Alice and its conflict with the apparatuses of state control eventually resulted in a massive wave of repression. It is these events that demonstrate very clearly how the media is a key site of struggle over the contemporary production of subjectivity, in Guattari's terms. Despite its apparent economic and technological backwardness at that time, Italy was the future of England, France and Germany. The molar aspect of this dynamic is that the polarisation of politics - into the mutually reinforcing duality of state violence and terrorism - was developed first of all in Italy before being applied elsewhere. This could be seen as embryonic of the global economy of fear under which we live today. However, what was driving this polarisation was the emergence of a new regime of consensus or control in which all previously existing forms of resistance such as trade unions or the communist party would be tolerated. Provided, that is, they fit into the overall regime of consensual control, for which they provide very useful tools for subjective reterritorialisation. The 'historic compromise' between the Italian communist party and the social democrats being just one example of this process. However, groups that still advocated violent rupture with this consensus would be hunted down and eliminated, with no pretense of liberal models of justice or legal rights, which was indeed what happened first in Italy and then in Germany. But Guattari isn't primarily interested in terror or state repression but rather the molecular revolution that was taking place around Radio Alice. A molecular revolution which the emerging consensual state apparatus was not able to tolerate. For Guattari, this was not a mere shift away from traditional apparatus of struggle, such as the communist party which have become completely compromised with the state, in favour of new micropolitical groupings such as Gay liberation or the Women's movement. These new groupings are no less susceptible to becoming reterritorialisations themselves: finding their institutional place in the manufacture of consensus. As Guattari puts it, 'there is a miniaturisation of forms of expression and of forms of struggle, but no reason to think that one can arrange to meet at a specific place for the molecular revolution to happen.'[5] While Guattari doesn't state it explicitly here, this corresponds very closely to the rejection of even micropolitical identities or political forms within the organisational autonomy enacted by Radio Alice. It was not just a question of giving space for excluded and marginalised subjects such as the young, homosexuals, women, the unemployed and others to speak but rather of generating a collective assemblage of enunciation allowing for the maximum of transversal connections and subjective transformations between all these emergent subjectivities. Guattari refers to Alice as a 'generalised revolution, a conjunction of sexual, relational, aesthetic and scientific revolutions all making cross-overs, markings and currents of deterritorialisation.'[6] Rather than pointing to a new revolutionary form, the experimentation of Radio Alice was a machine for the production of new forms of sensibility and sociability, the very intangible qualities constitutive of both the molecular revolution and the post-media era.

Guattari is somewhat more specific about these practices in the essay 'Popular Free Radio'.[7] In this essay he poses instead of the question of why Italy?, that of, why radio? Why not Super 8 film or cable TV? The answer is not technical but rather micropolitical. If media in their dominant usages can be seen as massive machines for the production of consensual subjectivity, then it is those media that can constitute an alternate production of subjectivity that will be the most amenable to a post-media transformation. Radio at this time had not only the technical advantage of lightweight replaceable technology, but more importantly was able to be used to create a self-referential feedback loop of political communication between producers and receivers, tending towards breaking down the distinctions between them:

> the totality of technical and human means available must permit the establishment of a veritable feedback loop between the auditors and the broadcast team: whether through direct intervention by phone, through opening studio doors, through interviews or programmes based on listener made cassettes.[8]

Again the experience of Radio Alice was exemplary in this regard:

> We realise [with Radio Alice] that radio constitutes but one central element of a whole range of communication means, from informal encounters in the Piazza Maggiore, to the daily newspaper – via billboards, mural paintings, posters, leaflets, meetings, community activities, festivals etc.[9]

In other words, it is less the question of the subversive use of a technical media form than the generation of a media, or rather post-media, ecology that is a self-referential network for an unforeseen processual production of subjectivity amplifying itself via technical means.

As Guattari points out, this is miles away from ideas of local or community radio in which groups should have the possibility on radio to represent their particular interests and from conventional ideas of political radio in which radio should be used as a megaphone for mobilising the masses. In contrast, on Alice, serious political discussions were likely to be interrupted by violently contradictory, humorous and poetico-delirious interventions and this was central to its unique micropolitics. It was even further removed from any modernist concern with perfecting either the technical form of radio (for example through concerns with perfecting sound quality) or its contents (the development and perfection of standard formats); listening to the tapes of Radio Alice is more than enough to convince about this last point! All of these other approaches to alternative radio, that is the local, the militant and the modernist, share an emphasis on specialisation; broadcasters set themselves up as specialists of contacts, culture and expression yet for Guattari, what really counts in popular free radio are 'collective assemblages of enunciation that absorb or traverse specialities.'[10]

What this type of radio achieved most of all was the short-circuiting of representation both in the aesthetic sense of representing the social realities they dealt with and in the political sense of the delegate or the authorised spokesperson, in favour of generating a space of direct communication in which, as Guattari put it,

> it is as if, in some immense, permanent meeting place – given the size of the potential audience – anyone, even the most hesitant, even those with the weakest voices, suddenly have the possibility of expressing themselves whenever they wanted. In these conditions, one can expect certain truths to find a new matter of expression.[11]

In this sense, Radio Alice was also an intervention into the language of media; the transformation from what Guattari calls the police languages of the managerial milieu and the university to a direct language of desire:

> direct speech, living speech, full of confidence, but also hesitation, contradiction, indeed even absurdity, is charged with desire. And it is always this aspect of desire that spokespeople, commentators and beaureaucrats of every stamp tend to reduce, to filter. [...] Languages of desire invent new means and tend to lead straight to action; they begin by 'touching,' by provoking laughter, by moving people, and then they make people want to 'move out,' towards those who speak and toward those stakes of concern to them.[12]

It is this activating dimension of popular free radio that most distinguishes it from the usual pacifying operations of the mass media. This also posed the greatest threat to the authorities; if people were just sitting at home listening to strange political broadcasts, or being urged to participate in conventional, organised political actions such as demonstrations that would be tolerable.

Once you start mobilising a massive and unpredictable political affectivity and subjectivation that is autonomous, self-referential and self-reinforcing, then this is a cause for panic on the part of the forces of social order, as was amply demonstrated in Bologna in 1977. Finally, in the much more poetic and manifesto-like preface with which Guattari introduces the translation of texts and documents from Radio Alice, he comes to a conclusion which can perhaps stand as an embryonic formula for the emergence of the post-media era as anticipated by Radio Alice and the Autonomia movement more generally:

> In Bologna and Rome, the thresholds of a revolution without any relation to the ones that have overturned history up until today have been illuminated, a revolution that will throw out not only capitalist regimes but also the bastions of bureaucratic socialism [...], a revolution, the fronts of which will perhaps embrace entire continents but which will also be concentrated sometimes on a specific neighbourhood, a factory, a school. Its wagers concern just as much the great economic and technological choices as attitudes, relations to the world and singularities of desire. Bosses, police officers, politicians, bureaucrats, professors and psychoanalysts will, in vain, conjugate their efforts to stop it, channel it, recuperate it, they will, in vain, sophisticate, diversify and miniaturise their weapons to the infinite, they will no longer succeed in gathering up the immense movement of flight and the multitude of molecular mutations of desire that it has already unleashed. The police have liquidated Alice – its animators are hunted, condemned, imprisoned, their sites are pillaged – but its work of revolutionary deterritorialisation is pursued ineluctably right up to the nervous fibres of its persecutors.[13]

This is because the revolution unleashed by Alice was not reducible to a political or media form but was rather an explosion of mutant desire capable of infecting the entire social field because of its slippery ungraspability and irreducibility to existing sociopolitical categories. It leaves the forces of order scratching their heads because they don't know where the crack-up is coming from since it doesn't rely on pre-existing identities or even express a future programme but rather only expresses immanently its own movement of auto-referential self-constitution, the proliferation of desires capable of resonating even with the forces of order themselves which now have to police not only these dangerous outsiders but also their own desires. This shift from fixed political subjectivities and a specified programme is the key to the transformation to a post-political politics and indeed to a post-media era in that politics becomes an unpredictable, immanent process of becoming rather than the fulfilment of a transcendental narrative. In today's political language one could say that what counts is the pure potential that another world is possible and the movement towards it rather than speculation as to how that world will be organised. As Guattari concludes:

> The point of view of the Alicians on this question is the following: they consider that the movement that arrives at destroying the gigantic capitalist-beaureaucratic machine will be, a fortiori, completely capable of constructing an other world – the collective competence in the matter will come to it in the course of the journey, without it being necessary, at the present stage to outline projections of societal change.[14]

Apart form anticipating many of the subsequent problematics of the counter-globalisation movement, what this citation tells us most of all about the post-media era is that it is not something that can be given in advance; it is instead a process of the production of subjectivity, the becoming of a collective assemblage of enunciation whose starting point is the emptiness and coerciveness of the normalising production that the mass media currently enact. This already gives us some indications as to what aspects of digital network culture might be able contribute to this emergence of a post-media sensibility and which elements, in contrast, merely help to add sophistication and diversity to normalisation processes under the guise of interactivity. However, to gain a different perspective on these questions we will now turn to the book by Berardi, *Félix*, which poses these exact problematics and constitutes the other side of the Guattari-Berardi, rhizomatic thought-media subversion encounter.

Félix, from the Encounter to Rhizomatic Thought

The first striking element of this book is its title, Félix not Guattari, thereby indicating that this is an intimate portrait, not an abstract account of a body of thought. The name Félix, of course, also has the meaning of happiness, which this book also poses as a directly political question. The subtitle too is also instructive: 'Narration of the encounter with the thought of Guattari, visionary cartography of the coming time.' This book is neither the personal, subjective account of Berardi's encounter with Guattari, nor an objective account of the latter's thought but rather something in between, a form of free indirect discourse in which Guattari himself and his thought will be situated both in relation to his own time and our own present that he didn't live to experience but anticipated through his rhizomatic and cartographic practice of thinking.

For the purposes of this essay the focus will be on the first part of the book, particularly those sections dealing directly with Berardi's encounter with Guattari, his account, influenced by Guattari of planetary psychopathology and especially the chapter entitled post-mediatic sensibility. It will not be an objective account of the latter's thought but rather something in between, a form of free indirect discourse in which Guattari himself and his thought will be situated both in relation to his own time and our own present that he didn't live to experience but anticipated through his rhizomatic and cartographic practice of thinking. The second part of the book provides a reading of all four of Guattari's works with Deleuze as well as his solo-authored *Chaosmosis* and argues strongly against the relative neglect of Guattari's contribution to the rhizomatic machine he constructed with Deleuze across the works they authored together. Berardi is in no way taking the opposite position of devaluing Deleuze, in fact he devotes a chapter of the book to one of the most concise and insightful accounts of Deleuze's thought without Guattari that one could find. Rather he insists that both thinkers constitute equal parts of a rhizomatic machine that was put into motion by their encounter and that leaving one half of this machine in shadow prevents any understanding of its functioning. However, it is the first part of the book that is most relevant to the encounter between Guattari and Berardi and the question of the post-media era that concerns us today.

The Encounter with Guattari from the Virtual to the Actual

If *Félix* comes out of the promise Berardi made on Guattari's death to write a book about his friend, the fact that it took eight years to complete gives some indication that the continuation, rather than the explication, of this thought is no straightforward task. Berardi points to some of the subsequent historical developments such as the development of the internet, the genome project and the development of the bio-informational paradigm, which each indicate the becoming-rhizome of the world that Guattari had been able to foresee and pre-map. Simultaneously, the thought of Deleuze and Guattari which, at the time of Guattari's death had a limited circulation, has gained a huge amount of attention especially on the internet from those involved with that form of collective enunciation known as the network. Finally, new political struggles over globalisation, beginning with the Seattle WTO protests in 1999, have demonstrated the political efficacy of this rhizomatic tendency. In Berardi's words, 'collective agents of rhizomatic enunciation and the insurrectional process are the same thing.'[15] On the plane of knowledge, there is the proliferation of ever more journals and books in the fields of philosophy, politics, psychoanalysis and aesthetics based around rhizomatic thought. All these, as well as those of biotechnology and cyberthought are thoroughly traversed by the concepts constructed by what Berardi calls the neo-logistic machine of Deleuze and Guattari.

Berardi's initial encounter with Guattari took place in a very different context, however, and was in the first instance a virtual one. Desperate to escape military service in 1974, Berardi decided to fake madness in order to be sent home. A French friend had told him of a psychoanalyst who 'was trying to see the world more from the schizo's point of view instead of that of psychiatry', and sent him one of his books, *A Tomb for an Oedipus Complex*.[16] Berardi used this text to help him falsify a schizo episode, in front of a medical colonel, who promptly sent him home thereby giving Berardi the impression that Guattari had saved him from the military barracks. The second virtual encounter also took place in confinement, this time in prison in 1976 under suspicion of having placed a bomb in the office of the Christian Democrats, when a friend handed him a copy of *Anti-Oedipus*. According to Berardi, 'it was within this map of existential and theoretical wandering that I lost myself that year. Proliferating and losing oneself, this was the sense of collective enterprise that the movement was attempting in Italy.'[17] On his release, and inspired by these perspectives, Berardi started with some friends the revue *A/Traverso: A Little Group in Multiplication* which would later lead to the formation of Radio Alice. Berardi acknowledges that the idea of contagion as a model of post-political organisation implied by this title was directly inspired by Guattari: 'the idea that social processes, political and cultural transformations are contagions, proliferations of viruses that spread out in the social body and produce mutations – here is an idea that emerged from Félix's molecular vision.'[18]

The actual encounter between Berardi and Guattari only happened in June 1977, after the creative insurrection that had taken place in Bologna around Radio Alice and the subsequent wave of repression had already been played out the preceding Spring. This worked out badly for Berardi who, from speaking at public meetings, meeting with other autonomists and publishing the *A/Traverso* journal, was accused of instigating class hatred and other crimes. In the meantime violent conflict had broken out in Bologna, as a result of the shooting of a young militant by the police, which was followed by a massive wave of arrests. Although in June Berardi, like many others, had fled to Paris, the Italian authorities had convinced the local police that he was a dangerous figure, and the anti-terror squad came to arrest him while on the way to have lunch with a girlfriend. This time, Guattari really acted to release him from captivity, mobilising the entire network of the Parisian intelligentsia. In a very short time Guattari's efforts created the conditions for Berardi's release and permission to remain in France. The very day of his release he went to Guattari's place and they wrote an appeal together against the repression in Italy and against the historic compromise between the Communist Party and the Christian Democrats, which would be subsequently signed by Gilles Deleuze, Michel Foucault, Roland Barthes, Julia Kristeva, Philippe Sollers and Jean-Paul Sartre and which had a substantial effect in Italy. This created the conditions for the convention against repression that took place in Bologna the following September, in which Guattari participated. While this was a massive and joyous event with tens of thousands of people participating, it also marked, for Berardi, the end of the movement in Italy and the drift towards the duality of terrorism and the state suppression of dissident social forces that it was unable to halt.

According to Berardi, it was as if everyone there was waiting for the 'magic word', capable of opening the path to a new history, a libertarian and egalitarian history that would avoid 'the backlash, violence, catastrophe, isolation and defeat of any solidarity.'[19] As Berardi puts it, they 'did not succeed in finding this magic word.'[20] In retrospect, Berardi says that something was botched, maybe even in the very idea of a convention against repression, therefore buying into negativity and dialectics rather than a meeting to affirm the creative power and capacities of the movement itself. Of course this would not have changed history whether on an Italian or a global scale where the furious capitalist counter-offensive, the imposition of Thatcherism, and the attacks on the form of life of the working class was already being prepared. But it might have helped transform a generation of rebels into autonomous experimenters.

While most of Berardi's subsequent contacts with Guattari concerned the problems of helping political expatriates from Italy and Germany in the wake of the rising tide of repression, Berardi claims that Guattari's philosophical creativity doesn't bear many traces of these defeats and the need to struggle for mere survival. Instead it 'succeeds in delineating a rather broad panorama of what our strength could today encompass. In this way, he sang the song of times that had to come.'[21] Following Guattari's death and during the radical shifts in the world from the fall of the Soviet Empire to the expansion of the global economy and the spreading of ethnic and religious conflicts, Berardi says he considered Guattari's rhizomatic thought as a map and tried to see the tracings of the real in continuity with the lines contained in this map. The map doesn't represent these developments but is rather a coexisting rhythm, an operation, a style which he seeks in this book to reconstruct and so to 'cause harmony to resonate among the chords, the refrains, and the dissonances in the contemporary planetary starting from that map.'[22]

La Depressione Félix or Overcoming the Felicist Hypocrisy

At this point, Berardi poses a crucial problem affecting rhizomatic thought and one of its major critiques; he states that the 'Félix Machine' attaches itself to the point of maximum openness of the provisory and nomadic community but doesn't accompany its dissolution. On a personal level this means dealing with the experience of depression, a subject which philosophy has tended semi-consciously to avoid as something which shouldn't be talked about publicly. In Guattari's work depression is not a subject but a voice as indicated by the title of his book on the 1980s, *The Years of Winter*. But not all the blame for depression can be ascribed to this winter since it is fundamental to desire itself. Berardi rather cryptically puts it like this: 'Desire is cruel, and so are autonomy, beauty, and the irresponsibility of dancing. Depression presents with the bill.'[23] Depression is intimately related to desire, in that it is both the dispersion of desire and the entropy against which desire and sense must struggle to exist. This is not only an affective condition but a directly political one that was experienced by a whole generation involved with militant struggle, with the collapse of all the new movements of the '60s and '70s in the context of the Realpolitik of Thatcherism and Reaganism. In works such as Anti-Oedipus with its Spinozist emphasis on the cultivation of joyful affects, there could be no place for such sad passions, which were instead associated with Oedipal repression and capitalist reterritorialisation (even the sad militant comes in for harsh treatment). However, as Berardi points out, there is also the time of depression, when the provisory community of desire, or the joyful creation of concepts, both of which are conglomerations of desiring energy no longer have a hold on the world which instead tends towards dispersion and dissolution. One could say that the affirmation of desiring-production in Anti-Oedipus has links with romanticism and the concept of *extasis* or pure expenditure, via Christian mysticism and Bataille; it is a youthful utopia. Berardi suggests that in Deleuze and Guattari's last work, *What is Philosophy?*, there is instead a senile utopia based around friendship rather than desire. This is formed in a markedly different social context in which there is a recognition of the illusions surrounding the idea of a revolutionary community of desiring production (Berardi compares this illusion to the Hindu concept of Maia and the Buddhist one of Samsara). But he claims that today we need neither a youthful nor a senile utopia but rather a sober cartography of the current conditions of the world, a cartography that Guattari undertook in the form of a prescient analysis of 'integrated world capitalism.' This concept which Berardi develops into one of planetary psychopathology rather than the now long dispersed psychedelic social utopia of *Anti-Oedipus* is the starting point for any emergent post-media sensibility. Berardi seems to be implying that while at the time Anti-Oedipus was not utopian since it was in direct contact with real social movements from '68 to autonomia, with the dispersal of these movements it takes on an atmosphere of utopian nostalgia.

Integrated World Capitalism and Planetary Psychopathology

The concept of integrated world capitalism, the idea that capitalism was re-organising itself on a global scale, is a commonplace today but when Guattari was first articulating it in the early 1980's it was almost a scandal. Political commentators at that time, while not seeing the Soviet bloc as a genuine social alternative, still saw the horizon of politics as defined by the dualist conflict between these two powers; a conflict that Guattari was prescient enough to see as a superficial mask for the real transformation in the direction of integrated world capitalism. The risk of nuclear holocaust which was the dominant theme in world politics at that time was of little interest to Guattari who saw instead the unleashing of a new '100 years war' along very different lines, predominantly between the privileged North and the excluded South, a prediction the truth of which has been more than confirmed by subsequent events.[24] More importantly than just prophesising globalisation, however, Guattari's concept of integrated world capitalism, contains an analysis not present in most discourses of globalisation, namely the recognition of capitalism not as an abstract category but as a semiotic operator. This means that the pervasiveness of capital is not dependent only on an effect of abstract overcoding mainly operative in the moment of exchange, but on the technologically mediated integration of the diverse moments of the production process from the project phase, to the informational and material phases. Capital becomes understood as an imposed or rather proliferated model understood as a semiotic operator, that is as a rule of generalised trans-codification. It also allows for the understanding of capital in relation to the new proliferations of margins, the residue of this process whether in the forms of diverse nationalisms and tribalisms (re-territorialisations) or minorities and subcultures (deterritorialisations).

Berardi takes this analysis further in his own concept of planetary psychopathology, which takes Guattari's concepts and places them in proximity with the contemporary world as transformed by the acceleration of globalisation and virtualisation processes since Guattari's death. Basically the world itself has become more clearly rhizomatic than it was previously. For example, one only has to look at the immediate relations between affects such as euphoria and depression and the contemporary functioning of the global stock exchange to see the direct investment of desire in the social field that Deleuze and Guattari anticipated in the 1970s. Of course the fluctuations of the stock market were always dependent on mass affectivity but the global interlinking of the world's economies coupled with the instantaneity of informational communications has turned it into a much more direct barometer of social desires.

For Berardi much of this situation corresponds to Guattari's concepts of mental ecology or ecosophy developed in his last book *Chaosmosis*. Taking inspiration from Bateson who claimed that there is 'an ecology of bad ideas just as there is an ecology of weeds', Guattari wanted to broaden ecology to deal not only with the natural atmosphere but also the mental atmosphere, arguing that these ecologies are inseparable.[25] For Berardi, this has been proven over the course of the '90s in which the rise of neoliberalism has had as a consequence not only devastating effects on the physical environment but the destruction of 'the psychic atmosphere in which humanity lives and communicates.'[26] Berardi goes so far as to claim that

> [t]he cultural devastation produced by neo-liberalism has upset social investments of desire, provoking a drought in productive social creativity and determining a true emotional plague, the aggression of everyone against everyone else, an obsessive fear of contact, a wave of Nazism without ideology, a purely visceral racism.[27]

This is the condition for the emergence of a planetary psychopathology to which both the monetary economy and new forms of infinite warfare are intimately linked (this would be Berardi's analysis in his most recent works such as *The Sage, The Merchant, The Warrior*, 2004).[28] This analysis, while seemingly far removed from Guattari's analysis of integrated world capitalism is in fact its direct extension in relation to perhaps the central domain of Guattari's thought namely schizoanalysis. Berardi acknowledges the extent to which his vision of the psychopathic global condition is indebted to Guattarian schizoanalysis in the following terms:

> Félix Guattari taught me to see social processes as the production of unconscious processes, and to see the unconscious as the laboratory in which the stages for social actions are produced. There is no need to think of power as a cold machine of decision and will. When one uses words like euphoria or panic or depression to describe the behaviour of the stock exchange or the markets, we must not think that this only is a question of metaphor. It is also a question of an adequate description of the psychopathology that traverses the social mind in a situation of informational overload and competitive stress.[29]

Disturbing as the devastation of the natural environment might be, the de-eroticisation of social relations in the direction of cold functionality, in which the other becomes perceived as a danger and potential factor of contagion (Berardi is making direct reference here to the HIV/AIDS crisis) is no less disturbing. Considering that the primary operator of this pathological subjectivation is the mass media, it is probably time to return to the problematic of the post-media era, which presents itself as the need to confront this drastically psychopathological or, at the very least, depressing situation.

Is there a Post-Mediatic Sensibility? Félix and Alice in Wonderland

At this point Berardi narrates the story of Guattari's involvement with and enthusiasm for Radio Alice and other free radio stations, a story in which he was 'very active.' He makes the point that unlike most critical thinkers with the exception of Walter Benjamin, Guattari had no fear of new technologies but rather embraced their potentials even when these had barely been developed. For example, he was enthusiastic about the communicative potentials of the net, well before the World Wide Web was developed and when his only experience of it was the rather primitive French Minitel system. According to Berardi, his thought was already a network thought even before the existence of the technical network. At this point he takes on the criticisms of Richard Barbrook who, from a state Marxist position, accuses Deleuze and Guattari (who he labels 'holy fools') of collusion with neoliberalism claiming that their thought operates by the same logic hence accounting for its popularity with Californian IT developers and enthusiasts of *Wired* magazine etc.[30] Berardi acknowledges that there is a link between high tech capitalism and rhizomatic thought even going so far as to accept the derogatory (for Barbrook) label of 'techno-nomadism'. The link is however not one of collusion but of adopting an immanent network approach to both critique and subversion. Berardi argues that it is this approach, rather than an outdated Marxist-Leninism, that has any potential for subversion over the reigning neoliberal high tech ideology because it is able to intervene in its own lines and rhythms of development, which completely leave behind the powers of conventional Marxist-Leninism. It is only through a mobile techno-nomadic thought that one is able to discern the possible lines of flight operative in the current world situation. As Guattari put it in *Chaosmosis*, 'democratic chaos which conceals a multitude of vectors of resingularisation, attractors of social creativity in search of actualisation. No question here of aleatory neo-liberalism, with its fanaticism for the market economy.'[31] According to Berardi, the free radio phenomenon was a kind of general proof of the existence of these vectors of re-singularisation, or attractors of social creativity. Today, of course, it is clear that this phenomenon was a direct precursor of the phenomenon of the internet model, which incarnates what Guattari called 'Postmediatic civil society.'[32] According to Berardi these free radios and especially Alice, based as it was on an explicit model of trans-semiotic communication and auto-organisation, 'anticipated a process of techno-communicative self-organisation prefiguring the end of the mediatic era. This awareness made Guattari a precursor of libertarian cyberculture.'[33] For Guattari, Radio Alice was not an instrument of information but a device for destructuration of the mediatic system aiming for the destructuration of the social nervous system, which in the succeeding decades has continued with effects of liberation but also of panic and catastrophe.

Perhaps we are at the point at which the question is no longer what is the post-media era, but rather what are the lines along which it will develop and what interventions are possible along these lines. Because if the post-mediatic era means the era of mass networks this is not in itself a positive development but one that holds as many catastrophic potentials as liberating ones. After all the spheres of both neoliberal economics and infinite warfare have also become rhizomatic and post-mediatic in their own way, even if this is very far from the future of the media era hoped for by Guattari. The question is one of how to compose networks of subjective auto-organisation that are able to assume an autonomy from neoliberal economic and military networks and their associated deadening of relationality, affect and desire in the direction of pure functionality and aggressivity. This evaluation in Guattari's work was expressed in terms of an ethico-aesthetic paradigm which saw in aesthetic practices indications of how networks might operate as vectors of resingularisation and the conjugation of singular events rather than instruments of normalisation and adjustment to the techno-economic-military exigencies of the neoliberal paradigm. It is in terms of this conflict between paradigms that the potentials for the post-media era envisaged by Guattari will continue to be played out and hopefully in some spheres actualised in an ethico-aesthetic auto-organisational direction.

Footnotes

1   Félix Guattari, 'Regimes, Pathways, Subjects', Gary Genosko (ed.), *The Guattari Reader*, Oxford/Cambridge Mass.: Blackwell, 1996, p.104.

2   Ibid, p.103.

3   Franco Berardi (Bifo), *Félix Guattari: Thought, Friendship and Visionary Cartography*, (trans. and eds.) Giuseppina Mecchia and Charles Stivale, New York/Hampshire: Palgrave Macmillan, 2008.

4   Félix Guattari, 'Why Italy?', John Johnston (trans.), in Sylvère Lotringer (ed.), *Soft Subversions*, New York: Semiotext(e), 1996, pp.79–84.

5   Ibid., p.82.

6   Ibid., p.84.

7   Félix Guattari, 'Popular Free Radio', in Sylvère Lotringer (ed.) *Soft Subversions*, New York: Semiotext(e), 1996, pp.73–78.

8   Ibid., p.74.

9   Ibid., p.75.

10   Ibid., p.75.

11   Ibid., p.76.

12   Ibid.

13   Félix Guattari, 'Préface: Des Millions et des Millions d'Alice en Puissance', Collectif A/Traverso. *Radio Alice, Radio Libre*. Paris: Delarge, 1978, p.11.

14   Ibid., pp.11–12.

15   Franco Berardi (Bifo), *Félix Guattari: Thought, Friendship and Visionary Cartography*,

Giuseppina Mecchia and Charles Stivale (trans. and eds.), New York/Hampshire: Palgrave Macmillan, 2008, p.1.

16   Ibid., p.2.
17   Ibid., p.3.
18   Ibid.
19   Ibid., p.4.
20   Ibid.
21   Ibid., p.5.
22   Ibid.
23   Ibid., p.9.
24   Ibid., pp.17–18.
25   Gregory Bateson, *Steps to an Ecology of Mind*, Chicago: Chicago University Press, p.492.
26   Franco Berardi, *Félix Guattari: Thought, Friendshp and Visionary Cartography*. Trans. and edited Giuseppina Mecchia and Charles J. Stivale. Houndsmills, Baisingstoke, New York: Palcgrave Macmillan, 2008, p.23.
27   Ibid., p.24.
28   *Il sapiente, il mercante, il guerriero: dal rifiuto del lavoro all'emergere del cognitariato* untranslated, *The Warrior, The Merchant, and the Sage: the Emergence of the Cognitariat Refusal of Work*, Rome: DeriveApprodi, 2004.
29   Berardi, 2008, op. cit. p.27.
30   Richard Barbrook, 'Holy Fools', in Josephine Berry Slater & Pauline van Mourik Broekman, *Proud To Be Flesh*, London: Mute Books, 2009. Available: http://www. imaginaryfutures.net/2007/04/14/the-holy-fools/
31   Félix Guattari, *Chaosmosis: An Ethico-Aesthetic Paradigm*, Paul Bains and Julian Pefanis (trans.), Sydney: Power Publications, 1992, p.117.
32   Berardi, 2008, op. cit., p.31.
33   Ibid.

THEORY OF THE SOVEREIGN MEDIA

ADILKNO

In this age of media overproduction, information immunity is a question of life or death. When the defence mechanism fails and the consumer is overwhelmed by strange impressions, doom seems near. To call a halt to crippling indifference, a media diet is prescribed. The pressure exerted on the world citizen to continually adapt his own image of the world and put technological innovations into practice puts him into a permanent state of insecurity. The urge to create disappears, and we are merely able to react to the overwhelming array of choices. Data are then no longer stimuli to interest, but an inimical barrage constituting a physical threat. From exchange to effacement: communication is preying on naked existence. The innocence of the media is no more. A period of stagnation will follow the rampant growth of the '80s. This is being foreshadowed by the propagation of a mentality of moderation. It is being made clear to us from all sides that we must stop handling information and images carelessly. Henceforth, the media and data traffic, like other sectors of Western society, must submit in their presentation to the diktat of ecology. The environment is more than endangered plants and animals. It is a mentality which, with abstract concepts like 'conservation' and 'recycling', sees the constructed media sphere as a third or fourth nature. Watchfulness prevails against all possible needless pollution and senseless waste.

Aware media users find a 'natural equilibrium' between receiving and transmitting information. After the euphoria of getting acquainted with the new technologies, they seek a balance between the immaterial environment, which evokes imaginary worlds, and the biographical one, where their own flesh lives. This balance is considered necessary to protect the pioneers in data land (who are working at the 'electronic frontier') from cold turkey. After the ecstasy of the emancipation phase we see a dissatisfaction in technoculture, and it may be seeking a destructive way out. High expectations all too easily end in great disappointment, which inspires hate for the machinery. Deleuze and Guattari would simply call it 'anti-production'; the sudden disgust that arises in those who have allowed themselves to be swept away in the stream of signs. Could this be the 'drama of communication' (freely adapted from Alice Miller), that at the moment we only receive and are sending no signals back? Or vice versa: putting too much data into the world, without getting anything back for it? Among data workers a feeling of emptiness and senselessness is arising, which can only temporarily be compensated for by the introduction of yet more new hard and software.

The sovereign media insulate themselves against the hyperculture. They seek no connection; they disconnect. This is their point of departure, we have lift-off. They leave the media surface and orbit the multimedia network as satellites. These doityourselfers shut themselves up inside a self built monad, an 'indivisible unit' of introverted technologies which, like a room without doors or windows, wishes to deny the existence of the world. This act is a denial of the maxim 'I am connected, therefore I am'. It conceals no longing for a return to nature. They do not criticise the baroque data environments or experience them as threats, but consider them material, to use as they please. They operate beyond clean and dirty, in the garbage system ruled by chaos *pur sang*.

Their carefree rummaging in the universal media archive is not a management strategy for jogging jammed creativity. These negative media refuse to be positively defined and are good for nothing. They demand no attention and constitute no enrichment of the existing media landscape. Once detached from every meaningful context, they switch over in fits and starts from one audio video collection to the next. The autonomously multiplying connections generate a sensory space, which is relaxing as well as nerve-racking. This tangle can never be exploited as a trend sensitive genre again. All the data in the world alternately make up one lovely big amusement park and a five star survival trek in the paranoid category, where humour descends on awkward moments like an angel of salvation and lifts the programme up out of the muck. Unlike the 'anti-media', which are based on a radical critique of capitalist (art) production, the sovereign media have alienated themselves from the entire business of politics and the art scene. An advanced mutual disinterest hampers any interaction. They move in parallel worlds which do not interfere with each other. No anti-information or criticism of politics or art is given in order to start up a dialogue with the authorities. Once sovereign, media are no longer attacked, but tolerated and, of course, ignored. But this lack of interest is not a result of disdain for the hobbyist amateur or political infantilism; it is the contemporary attitude towards any image or sound that is bestowed on the world anyway.

Sovereign media are equipped with their own starters and do not need to push off from any possible predecessors or other media. They are different from the post'68 concept of alternative media and from the autonomous 'inside' media of the '80s. The alternative media work on the principle of 'anti-publicity' and mirror the mainstream media, which they feel needs to be corrected and supplemented. This strategy aims to make the individual aware of his behaviour as well as his opinion. This process will ultimately be seen in a changed public opinion. These little media have no general claims but work with a positive variant of the cancer model, which assumes that in the long term everyone, whether indirectly or through the big media, will become informed about the problem being broached. They presuppose a tight network stretched around and through society, so that in the end the activism of a few will unleash a chain reaction by many. Until that time, they direct themselves at a relatively small group, in the certainty that their info will not stay stuck in a ghetto or start feeding back in the form of internal debates. This 'megaphone model' aims in particular at liberal left opinion leaders, who have no time to accumulate information or invent arguments and get politically motivated specialists to do this thankless work. Movements in the '60s and '70s gave themes like feminism, the third world and the environment a great range this way. Professionalisation and market conformism in those circles, however, have caused people to switch to the 'real' media. The laboratories where information and argumentation get tested are currently an inseparable part of the media manufacturing process, now that their movements have become just as virtual as the media they figure in.

At the end of the '70s, radicals who had gotten tired of waiting for the other's change of consciousness founded the so-called 'inside media'. At precisely the moment that the official media started emancipating themselves and terms like 'press' and 'public opinion' vanished from the scene, a group of activists gave up the belief in their deaf fellow citizens and got to work themselves. Although to unknowing outsiders they seemed a continuation of the alternative media activity, they let go of the cancer model and, like the official media, went gliding. The mirror of the alternative media was crushed. It had become pointless to keep appealing to public responsibility; they needed to look for a different imaginary quantity to concentrate on: 'the movement'.

Although they were only locally available, they had no concern for the regional restriction which the ascending local media impose upon themselves. They no longer wanted to be alternative city papers. In form as well as content they became transnational, like their global peers. They wanted nothing to do with growth. Their brilliant dilettancy turned out to be not a childhood illness, but an essential component. As a leftover product of vanished radical movements, which flare up every now and then, their continuity and unchangingness remain breathtaking to this day. It cannot be reduced to their dogma. They turn away from the short media time and create their own space-time continuum.

The sovereign media are the cream of all the missionary work performed in the media galaxy. They have cut all surviving imaginary ties with truth, reality and representation. They no longer concentrate on the wishes of a specific target group, as the 'inside' media still do. They have emancipated themselves from any potential audience, and thus they do not approach their audience as a moldable market segment, but offer it the 'royal space' the other deserves. Their goal and legitimacy lie not outside the media, but in practicable 'total decontrol'. Their apparently narcissistic behaviour bears witness to their being sure of themselves, which is not broadcast. The signal is there; you only have to pick it up. Sovereign media invite us to hop right onto the media bus. They have a secret pact with noise, the father of all information. And time is not a problem there is room for the extended version as well as the sampled quotation. This is only possible through the grace of no-profile. Without being otherwise secretive about their own existence, the sovereigns remain unnoticed, since they stay in the blind spot that the bright media radiation creates in the eye. And that's the reason they need not be noticed as an avant-garde trend and expected to provide art with a new impetus. The reason sovereign media are difficult to distinguish as a separate category is because the shape in which they appear can never shine in its full lustre. The programme producers don't show themselves; we see only their masks, in the formats familiar to us. Every successful experiment that can possibly be pointed to as an artistic or political statement is immediately exposed to contamination. The mixers inherently do not provoke, but infect chance passers by with corrupted banalities which present themselves in all their friendly triviality. An inextricable tangle of meaning and irony makes it impossible for the experienced media reader to make sense of this.

The atmosphere inside the sealed cabin conflicts with the ideology of networking. As a central co-ordination machine, the computer subjects all old media to the digital regime. The sovereign media, conversely, make their own kind of connections, which are untranslatable into one universal code. High-tech is put to the test and turned inside out. But this trip to the interior of the machine does not result in a total multimedia art work. Disbelief in the total engagement of the senses and technically perfect representation is too great for that. The required energy is simply generated by short-circuits, confusion of tongues, atmospheric disturbances and clashing cultures. Only when computer driven networks begin to break their own connections, and scare off their potential users, will it be time for the sovereigns to log in.

FROM POST-MEDIA TO POST-MEDIUM: RETHINKING ONTOLOGY IN ART AND TECHNOLOGY

CADENCE KINSEY

Recent discussions of computer based artistic practices have tended to focus on the relationship between the 'real' and the 'virtual' – invoking the problematic binary even while they attempt to undo it – and the destabilisation of the referent in digital image production. In discussions related to computer technologies the idea of code and, specifically, binary has been a central focus of critical attention as the common feature to all. As a series of 1s and 0s, binary was perceived as a form of representation that made it all too easy for the new information-image to be cut, pasted, transformed and generated from nothing; an endless proliferation of digitally manipulated images, no longer attached to the material and political terrain of 'the real'. This precipitated a crisis in theories of human-machine interaction around the mid-'90s, which saw numerous theorists attempting to map a supposedly disembodied interaction with this abstract plane of representation comprised of code.[1] Such ideas further intersected with the then emergent knowledge of genetics, resulting in a perceived equivalence between binary and genetic code that aggravated the critical discourse to the point where the human subject (whatever that may have been) was also considered to be in a state of crisis.[2] DNA, like text, could also be 'cut' and 'pasted' to produce new formations. Even in recent art practices that utilise the techniques of genetic engineering, such as Eduardo Kac's *The Eighth Day* (2001), equivalence between different codes (language, genetics, binary) is frequently assumed and reinforced.[3]

The way in which binary code appears to operate thus establishes one of the primary instances of western dualism that the discourses of feminism and science & technology studies have hoped to undo: that between information and materiality (and subsequently the correlative binaries transcendence/immanence, and presence/absence). These tenacious ideals are, of course, founded upon the Boolean logic of western epistemology.[4] That the world is not only structured *like* but particularly *through* language means that, beyond the simple iconic mapping of the written digits '1' and '0' onto biological sex in the work of Sadie Plant, the relationship between binary code and western binaries is perhaps most acutely felt in the realm of representation.[5] As a displacement of the 'flow' of analogue signals, the discrete 'packets' or 'pulses' of binary represent a supposedly universal mode of representation in which information can be successfully conveyed across a range of material substrates, without loss or change. As such, the discourse of what has been termed, variously, as 'Net.Art', 'New Media Art', 'Digital Art', and 'Internet Art' is often filtered through this postmodernist detachment of signifier from signified, rubbing out the tension between 'figure' and 'ground' at the heart of modernist theories of representation. Such a filtering has historically only served to repeat the rhetoric of equivalency that has sustained the critique of digital technology from within late capitalism, vis a vis Baudrillard, who wrote in 1981 that the problem with everything being a system of signs is that they 'lend themselves to all systems of equivalence, all binary oppositions and all combinatory algebra' in the production of a 'perfect descriptive machine'.[6]

This, of course, is a problem of much art historical writing about practices that work with the digital, rather than the practices themselves. For example, while the use of plagiarism by early net.artists has been theorised by writers such as Stewart Home as a counter to the technique of appropriation in the postmodernist image economy outlined above, since plagiarism necessarily emphasises points of both material contiguity and disconnection in the transferral of information, art history has tended to emphasise the immateriality of digital practices. This both unfolds onto notions of equivalency in considerations of medium as an ontological category, and effaces the way in which these practices were actually attempting to work through the heterogeneous conditions that inflected upon the circulation of information online. That computer based artistic practices have been grouped and held together under a variety of neologisms, such as 'New Media Art', which tacitly support particular categories of media, speaks to a degree of technological determinism. As such, it highlights both the necessity of attempting to write about technology's relation to art more generally, and the potential problematics of doing so. For example, 'optical' or 'retinal' art from the 1960s tends to be read as determined by technological innovation and scientific progress. As a result of this association with mechanical modes of image production, such works are often mapped onto modernist notions of the autonomy of medium, and subsequently to models of 'disembodied' spectatorship.[7] Such readings, as one might expect, tend to be dismissed as both reductive and ideologically informed.[8]

However, what the critical rhetoric against techno-determinism assumes is that technology even has a stable identity that may oppose and stultify 'art'. Working with the assumption that the plethora of aesthetic categories from 'Net.Art' to 'New Media Art' might actually suggest a fundamental instability in – rather than reification of – the ontology of digital technology, this paper looks at the way in which the rhetoric of 'post-media' has been mapped onto the art historical notion of 'post-medium', through the work of Rosalind Krauss and her reading of Marcel Broodthaers. Through this mapping I hope to demonstrate that the liberating potentiality

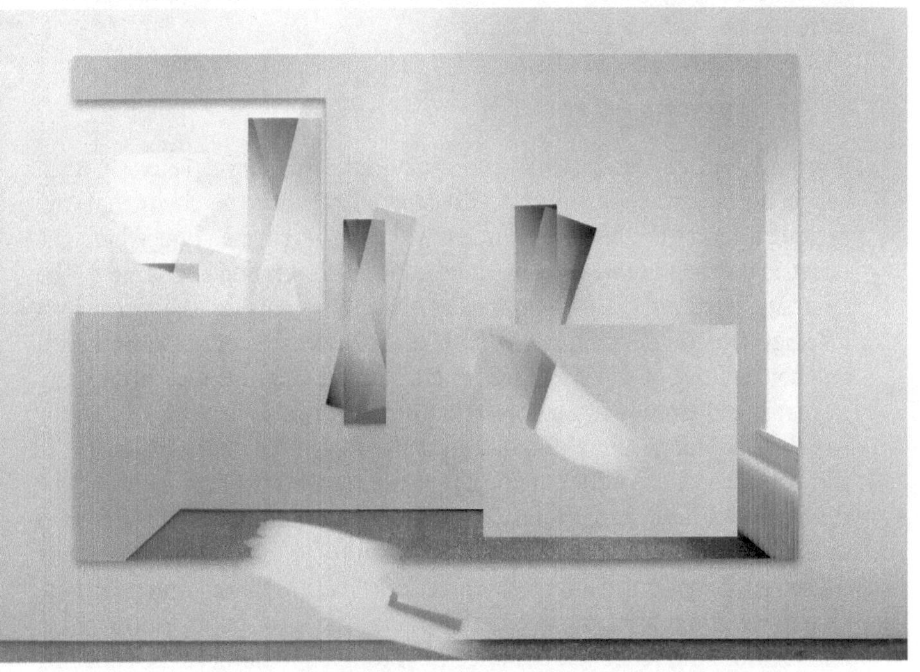

Artie Vierkant, *Image Objects*, 2011-present, UV prints on sintra, altered documentation images. Image courtesy the artist.

of information exchange, founded on a lateral equivalence of media and so crucial to the work of Guattari and early net.artists, actually collapses back into the hegemonic structures of capital when it is taken up by the discursive networks of art history, which reads the notion of equivalence in relation to postmodernist theories of the circulation of images. Thus, exploring the way in which an indeterminate ontology of technology has both constituted, and been constituted by, an indeterminate ontology of art at several key historical moments, including the mid- to late 1960s and late 2000s, which witnessed key shifts in categories of media, this essay will re-examine post-media as an aesthetic proposition for 2013.

***

Working within the discursive context outlined above, Felix Guattari began his 1990 text 'Towards a Post-Media Era' with the claim that 'the digitalization of the television image will soon reach the point where the television screen is the same as the computer screen and the same as the telematic receiver'.[9] However, rather than emphasising the pernicious ideology of equivalence fostered within the discourses of postmodernism and constitutive of the structures of late capital, Guattari was attempting to map a redemptive re-appropriation of both media – as the ground for the flow of information – and *the* media. In laterally conjoining media through a rejection of their material specificity, Guattari paradoxically saw the potential interchangeability of digital systems of representation, such as the TV or computer screen, as an opportunity to foster a heterogeneous collection of 'molecular, alternative practices'. Thus, in the discourses of post-media, the removal of the alienating properties of media, its normalising and pressurising tendencies, is effected through a removal of the concerns of the material and the indexical, in other words the analogue which, for Guattari, had become overcoded in its association with a mythological 'real'. In the context of artistic practice, the possibilities and the problems that this idea potentially unfolds onto are vast. In an attempt to reject the annexing of 'art and technology' from the concerns of art history more generally, I want to argue that the question of post-media is pertinent not just in relation to recent artistic practices that engage with digital technology, but also, crucially, the histories and theories of modernism and conceptualism.

This can, of course, be seen in the mapping of the concept of post-media onto the art historical notion of post-medium. Rosalind Krauss published her lecture on Marcel Broodthaers, 'A Voyage on the North Sea: Art in the

Age of the Post-Medium Condition', some ten years after Guattari's article first appeared in French. Citing the examples of film and video in relation to conceptualism, Krauss argued that an understanding of medium as 'aggregative', that is to say as a fundamentally heterogeneous structure of interlocking supports and conventions, could be used to displace the essentialising tendencies of Greenbergian modernism. Such an assertion not only presented the possibility that the specificity of mediums need no longer be attached to, or collapsed into, the physicality of their support, but also that it is precisely through the emergence of new technologies, such as video, that a space of indeterminacy was opened up in which to rethink artistic and discursive categories.

Indeed, Krauss argued that it was the development of the Portapak video camera and monitor system in 1968 that 'shattered' traditional notions of medium specificity.[10] In part, this was achieved through an intensification of the theories developed in relation to film, particularly structuralist film-making as promoted by Jonas Mekas at the Anthology Film Archives. Although early structuralist film sought to reduce the various constituent components of film to a singular form, later work argued that the very existence of such varied components actually suggested a fundamental heterogeneity of medium. Thus, models of film developed in the late 1960s and early 1970s allowed a slightly later generation of artists to think about the specificity of film not in relation to the celluloid strip of images, nor the camera that filmed them, nor the projector, nor the beam of light that relays the images to the screen, nor the screen itself, but in relation to a compound idea of 'apparatus'.[11]

For Krauss, it was the work of Broodthaers that first demonstrated this particular conception of medium; describing a specificity of film that was 'self-differing', in that it was able to contain the paradoxical interrelationships between 'simultaneity and sequence, [and the] layering of sound or text over image' that is found in film.[12] Importantly for Krauss however, this aggregate ontology of the filmic apparatus was only fully theorised after the development of video, which from the outset had been tied to the discourses of systems, information theory and media ecology.[13] In her work on post-medium, Krauss thus speaks to the question of equivalency and interchangeability raised by Guattari's notion of post-media on several counts. Not only is an equivalence between the aggregative specificity of the different formats of film and video being established but, furthermore, so too is a conceptual economy that displaces the distinction between figure and ground, signifier and signified. She writes,

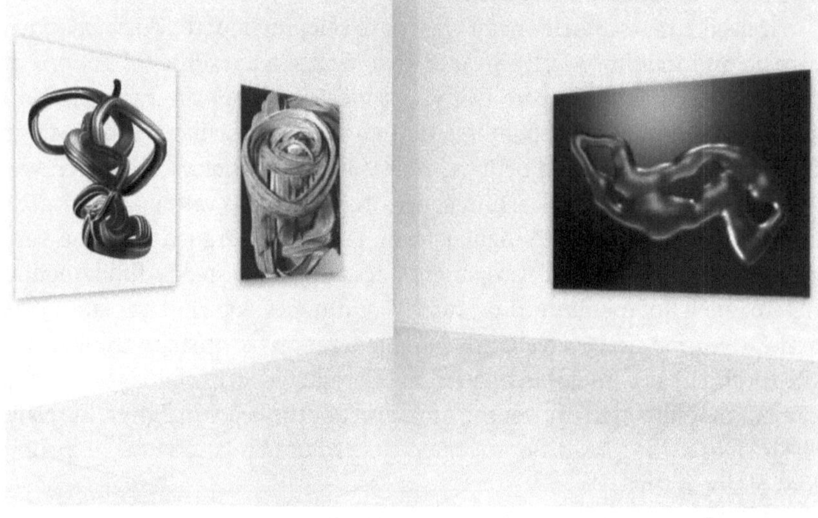

Paint FX (Jon Rafman, Parker Ito, Micah Schippa, Tabor Robak, John Transue), *Untitled*, 2010, digital painting. Image courtesy the artists.

Broodthaers scattered the image of the eagle across a multiplicity of sites, so that every material support, including the site itself – whether art magazine, dealer's fair booth, or museum gallery – will now be leveled, reduced to a system of pure equivalency by the homogenizing principle of commodification, the operation of pure exchange value from which nothing can escape and for which everything is transparent to the underlying market for which it is a sign.[14]

Theorising medium outside of its material or physical support, and instead emphasising the interlocking and interdependent structures that comprise it, suggests that representation ought to be understood as a system of image-signs that have become both inherently decontextualised but also reliant on several *different* contexts or frames simultaneously. In many ways, therefore, Krauss' reading of the post-medium condition of conceptualism is a descendent of her work on the medium of video. In her foundational article 'Video: the Aesthetics of Narcissism', published in 1976, Krauss identified video's defining property as 'liveness', of allowing the performer to watch him/herself *as if in a mirror*. Importantly, this was perceived by Krauss as being fundamentally *psychological* rather than *physical* in nature, since the medium was structured around what she saw as a narcissistic doubling of the self, in which 'the self' referred either to the body of the artist in the case of works on tape, or the body of the spectator in video installations.[15] Likening the medium of video to the 'mediums' of parapsychology, in which the human body becomes both a sender and receiver of communications that arise from an invisible source, Krauss' work suggests that the image is little more than a sign that can *pass through* a range of physical supports without change or alteration. By defining the medium of video as psychological, Krauss inserted the emergent discourse around video into a genealogy of thought that considered the flow of information (which historically includes human thought processes) as removed from the material substrates through which they flow. As such, Krauss inserts the image-as-information into the canon of western metaphysics, as described so lucidly by N. Katherine Hayles in her important work *How We Became Posthuman: Virtual Bodies in Cybernetics, Literature and Informatics* (1999).

Drawing on archival material from the Macy Conferences, held in New York in the immediate post-war period (1946-53), Hayles looked at the relationship between the gendered body and socio-cultural constructions of informational systems from the last 50 years, noting the implications for themes of transcendence in VR (virtual reality) models of a disembodied subject, and how that might be seen to replicate the liberal subject of the enlightenment. Hayles notes that Norbert Weiner's original work on feedback systems – formalised as the field of 'cybernetics', a term deriving from the Greek for 'steersman' – defined information as an entity distinct from the substrates carrying it, subsequently producing a conceptualisation of information as a kind of 'bodiless fluid' that could flow between different substrates without any loss or change. Any models trying to account for the embodiedness of the technological subject was therefore troubled by this definition, as human identity became increasingly associated with 'thinking machines'. In other words, extending the legacy of the cogito, thought was conceived as more like an informational pattern than an embodied enaction.[16] Equivalency and interchangeability are therefore at the heart of Krauss' work on both medium and post-medium, which video somehow seems to sit between in its influence on conceptualism, since they provide a clear iteration of the way in which a postmodern detachment of signifier from signified has been mapped onto a conceptual detachment between figure and ground in the field of representation. As noted in the introduction, such claims have intensified in relation to the increasingly widespread use of digital technology, and are precisely what Guattari was attempting to work against with his model of heterogenous, molecular practices that would reject hierarchical top down structures of information transfer and broadcast in favour of laterally conjoined moments of exchange.

Confronted with new modes of artistic practice and new techniques and technologies of representation, Krauss appears to have framed her work on medium with the inter-related discursive structures of postmodernism and information theory. Reading the image-as-information in this way, Krauss' work both reflects and constitutes a very particular cultural narrative in which the image, and the correlative representational structures of language, binary and genetics, have been theorised in relation to postmodernist notions of equivalency. There is, furthermore, a sense in which the authority of this model of technology has been presupposed in order to construct a position of stability against which to test out the instability of emergent artistic categories. What I am suggesting is that the treatment of medium in the history of art has been marked by cultural narratives around technology, which, in turn, are then used to substantiate those very claims about technology. Indeed, it has only been in the last 10-15 years that a narrative of the digital has even emerged to counter notions of equivalency and interchangeability.[17] By contrast, I want to argue that the indeterminacy of categories of media that emerged in the late 1960s, which Krauss touches on in relation to the work of Broodthaers, actually speaks to an indeterminacy in the ontology of technology during this period, which should neither be countered by, nor used to counter, the troubling of artistic categories. Although Broodthaers' heterogeneous practice offered Krauss a ready platform from which to expand on the ways in which conceptualism had already problematised questions of medium at the time, I would like to argue for an alternative moment in which artistic practice was able to foreground this indeterminate ontology in both art and technology, and resist a collapse back into secure categories coded through the notion of 'medium'.[18]

Between 1966 and 1971 in New York City, technology not only mediated an engagement with painting but, in many cases, was actually seen as constitutive of a painterly practice. For example, in 1966, Andy Warhol collaborated on his installation *Silver Clouds* with Billy Kluver, an electrical engineer at Bell Laboratories and co-founder of E.A.T. Although they were made from Scotchpak, a metalised plastic film that had been recently developed by 3M, Warhol described these 'clouds' or 'pillows' as paintings. Similarly, Jo Baer linked the compositional arrangement of her painting *Untitled (White Square with Lavender)* (1964-1967) with the perceptual theories of Austrian Physicist Ernst Mach in an article in *Aspen*; Roy Liechtenstein used Ben-Day dots, a commercial printing technique, in both his paintings and his important film installation *Three Landscapes* (1971); Carolee Schneemann described her film *Fuses* (1967) as painting; and Barnett Newman said that Dan Flavin had been 'painting with lights'.

That technology could be both read as painting and influenced by it was only possible because of the relatively indeterminate status that technology held during this period, as new technologies were rapidly developed and abandoned (computer interface hardware, VHS, Betamax). Indeed, this indeterminacy has been productively investigated elsewhere and in other contexts, for example with regards the importance of video for feminist artists precisely because it lacked a critical history and pre-defined discourse.[19] What these projects seem to demonstrate is that it was not necessary to work with painting as a *medium* in order to be critically invested in its concerns as a *material* practice, and that technology offered a space from which such concerns could be investigated. Equally, such practices illustrated the fact that the ontologies of both art and technology were becoming fundamentally destabilised during this period and that, as per Guattari's conception of post-media, this was a potentially liberating, generative moment in which to reclaim and shift broader cultural narratives related to art and technology.

As such, these works represent early test cases that actually run parallel to conceptualism in their attempt to negotiate the questions of medium raised within the high modernism of Clement Greenberg and 1950s abstraction. Unlike the conceptual practices of Broodthaers and Joseph Kosuth, which, as Krauss has demonstrated, mapped the question of medium and subsequently post-medium through the structures of language, the relationship between painting and technology outlined above speaks to a condition of art that equally emphasises representation and its ground, and an ontology of technology that is neither determined nor deterministic. Categories of medium are destabilised in these practices not in order to divest themselves of the contingency and specificity of their material support, but rather to ask questions of medium beyond the limited frameworks provided by high modernism.

This destabilising of the discursive categories of art history and categories of media represents a point of contiguity between the historical practices outlined above and recent work with the digital that has emerged from 2011 onwards. Currently, there is a significant network of artists and organisations in Europe and North America working in a mode described as internet 'aware', or 'post-internet', art. These individuals and groups are engaged in important practice based research questions concerning the interrelationships between technology, representation and capital. What is important about such practices is that, in the context of thinking post-medium through post-media, artists working 'after the Internet' do not necessarily situate their practice online, nor do they work exclusively with the digital, even while they are critically invested in it. Instead, these practices straddle a variety of media – including painting, performance, writing, installation and analogue technologies – posing questions beyond the traditional discourses of art and technology, which actually extends something of the mode of working in the mid-'60s outlined above. For example, Artie Vierkant's *Image Objects* project (2011 onwards), which consists of giant, acid-coloured UV prints on sintra, sit somewhere between physical objects and altered digital images, prompting questions of materiality in relation to digital culture.[20] While, conversely, the group PaintFX (consisting of Jon Rafman, Parker Ito, John Transue, Micah Schippa, and Tabor Robak) make digital images in which a mimicry of the formal and material properties of paint is always already apparently inflected through the digital.

Importantly, one of the ways in which these practices effect an engagement with the discourses of technology is precisely through a reversal of the strategies of conceptualism, which emphasised *text* over *context*. There

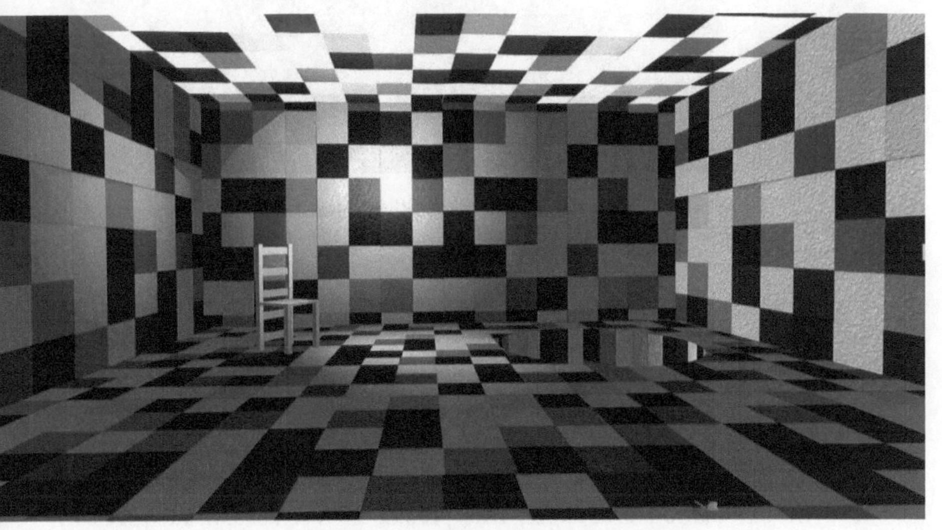

Jon Rafman, *BNPJ.exe*, 2011, realtime 3D environment.
Image courtesy the artist.

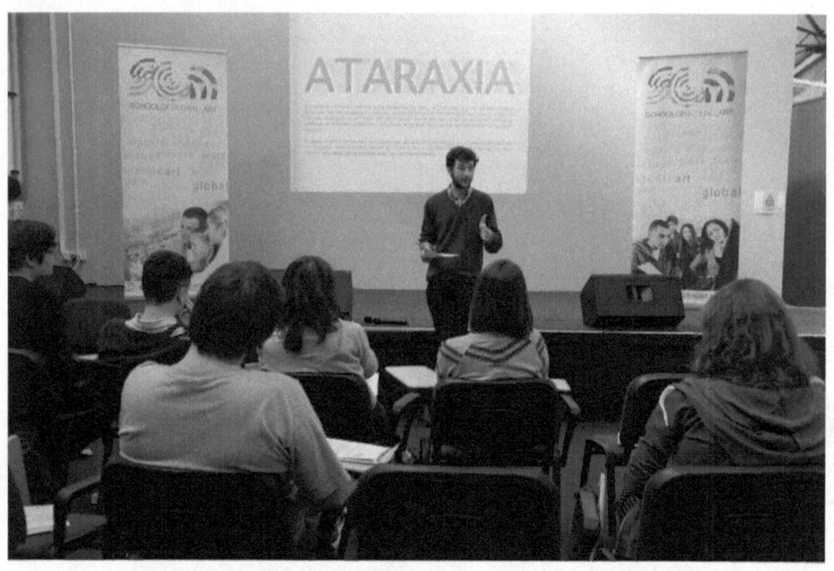

LuckyPDF (John Hill, James Early, Ollie Hogan, Yuri Pattison),
School of Global Art, 2012, workshop. Image courtesy the artists.

is now a widespread emergence of an investigation into the context in which images, practices and ideas are circulating, rather than into the images, practices and ideas themselves. Although Rafman's *BNPJ.exe* (2011) project, in which a navigable 3D space is entirely papered in textures taken from foundational works of the history of art (prompting cease and desist letters from Sodrac, ARS and ADAGP), could be read in the context of appropriation and the circulation of images, this project in fact asks what, precisely, remains of the digital through which to constitute and meaningfully contextualise the image. Further, and related to this, the practice of Ed Fornieles, Lucky PDF and Arcadia_Missa is premised on the establishment of curatorial or conceptual frames for other practitioners to work within. Such projects bring urgent questions of cultural appropriation, agency, and artistic production in the digital age to the fore, and are notable for playing on – and into – the ideologies of carefully chosen institutional 'frameworks', from the art school (LuckyPDF, *School of Global Art*, 2012), to the office (Arcadia_ Missa, *Open Office*, 2012) to Facebook (Fornieles, *Character Date*, 2012; *Dorm Daze*, 2011). In much the same way as the ontology of painting troubled, and was troubled by, technology in the late 1960s, so too have recent practices situated themselves beyond traditional categories of medium. However, the purpose of this has not been to reject a specificity of medium, which would fold back into those discursive frameworks in which text is privileged over context, but rather to open up new lines through which to interrogate what it is that now constitutes that very specificity. In other words, these practices actually retain medium as a central question even while they use the framework of post-medium to work outside of its established categories.

The development of video technology and information theory in the late 1960s and Web 2.0 technology in the mid 2000s thus mark two moments in which post-medium emerges as a central term for engaging with artistic practice. During both these periods, the emergent ontology of technology not only destabilised previously secure categories of artistic 'media' and their relation to the notion of 'medium', but were themselves made increasingly unstable. However, art history has tended to treat the discourses of technology as deterministic, which has, in turn, suggested that technology is itself determined about its own identity. This is clearly demonstrated by the way in which Krauss' model of post-medium invokes a category of equivalency that has been ultimately derived from the detachment of the digital and the material in information theory. By contrast, looking beyond the question of post-medium as raised by conceptualism, I propose that there are a number of practices that engage with traditional categories of media, such as painting, in order to emphasise and sustain a fundamental disruption in the ontology of both art and technology. Such practices are not only able to call the notion of medium into question as a determining category for art history, but also have the potential to help displace the instrumentalising narratives of technology in favour of questions of contingency and materiality. For these particular sets of practices, post-medium is thus mobilised as a liberating framework through which to reject the claim that the concerns of technology are antithetical to the concerns of art, reclaiming a questioning of the specificity of mediums that might operate beyond the discourses of high modernism.

Footnotes

1   Kevin Robins, 'The Virtual Unconscious in Postphotography', *Electronic Culture: Technology and Visual Representation*, Timothy Druckrey, (ed.), New York: Aperture, 1996, pp.154–163; Steven Johnson, *Interface Culture: How New Technology Transforms the Way We Create and Communicate*, San Francisco: HarperCollins, 1997; Lucia Sommer, 'In/Visible Body: Notes on Biotechnologies' Vision', *Domain Errors! Cyberfeminist Practices*, F. Wilding, M. Fernandez, M. M. Wright (eds.), New

York: Autonomedia, 2002, pp.23-133.

2   Donna Haraway, 'Biopolitics of Postmodern Bodies: Determinations of Self in Immune System Discourse', *Knowledge, Power, Practice: The Anthropology of Medicine and Everyday Life*, S. Lindenbaum and M. Lock (eds.), Berkeley, LA and London: University of California Press, 1993, pp.364-410; Catherine Waldby, 'The Visible Human Project: Data into Flesh, Flesh into Data', *Wild Science: Reading Feminism, Medicine and the Media*, J. Marchessault and K. Sawchuk (eds.), London and New York: Routledge, 2000 (pp.24-38); John Avise, *The Hope, Hype and Reality of Genetic Engineering*, Oxford and New York: Oxford University Press, 2004; Eugene Thacker, 'Open Source DNA and Bioinformatics Bodies', *Signs of Life: Bioart and Beyond*, Eduardo Kac (ed.), Cambridge MA: MIT Press, 2006, pp.31-42; Eugene Thacker, 'Data Made Flesh: Biotechnology and the Discourse of the Posthuman', *Cultural Critique*, No. 53, Posthumanism, 2003, pp.72-97.

3   S. Britton and D. Collins (eds.), *The Eighth Day: The Transgenic Art of Eduardo Kac*, Institute for Studies in the Arts: Arizona State University, 2003.

4   The reference to Boolean logic is here key. In his masters thesis of 1937, Claude Shannon explicitly related the binary functioning of digital electronic circuitry to the and/or operators theorised by George Boole. See Claude Shannon, 'A Symbolic Analysis of Relay and Switching Circuits', unpublished masters thesis, MIT, 1937.

5   Sadie Plant, *Zeros and Ones: Digital Women and the New Technoculture*, New York: Doubleday, 1997.

6   Jean Baudrillard, 'Simulacra and Simulations', *Baudrillard: Selected Writings*, M. Poster, (ed.), Cambridge: Polity Press, 1998, pp.166-184, p.167.

7   Gerald Oster and Yasumouri Nishijima, 'Moiré Patterns', in *Scientific American*, 1963, pp.54-63; William Seitz, *The Responsive Eye*, ex. cat., New York: Museum of Modern Art New York, 1965; Rosalind Krauss, 'Afterthoughts on Op', *Art International* vol. 9, no. 5, 1965, pp.75-76.

8   For an account of this in relation to Op Art, see Pamela Lee, 'Bridget Riley's Eye/ Body Problem', *October* Vol. 98, 2001, pp.26-46.

9   Félix Guattari 'Towards a Post-Media Era', A. Sebti, A. & C. Apprich. (trans.), published online February 2012 http://www.metamute.org/editorial/lab/towards-post-media-era

10   Rosalind Krauss, *A Voyage on the North Sea: Art in the Age of the Post-Medium Condition*, London: Thames and Hudson, 2000 p.24.

11   J.-L. Baudry, 'The Apparatus', *Camera Obscura*, No.1, 1976; T. de Lauretis and S. Heath (eds), *The Cinematic Apparatus*, London: Macmillan, 1980.

12   Krauss, 2000, op cit p.45.

13   On this see David Joselit, 'Art as Information: Systems, Site, Media' in *American Art Since 1945*, London: Thames and Hudson, 2003, pp.129-159; David Joselit, 'Tale of the Tape: *Radical Software*' in in *Art and the Moving Image: a Critical Reader*, T. Leighton, (ed.), London: Tate Publishing, 2008, pp.220-227.

14   Krauss, 2000, op. cit. p.15.

15   Krauss, 'Video: the Aesthetics of Narcissism' in *October*, Vol. 1, 1976, pp.50-64.

16   N Katherine Hayles, *How We Became Posthuman: Virtual Bodies in Cybernetics, Literature and Informatics*, Chicago and London: University of Chicago Press, 1999.

17   See Hayles and Wendy Chun, *Programmed Visions: Software and Memory*, Cambridge, Mass: MIT Press, 2011.

18   On the way in which Conceptualisim had already destabilised categories of media, see Lucy Lippard, *Six Years: the Dematerialization of the Art Object from 1966 to*

1972 (1973) University of California Press 1997.
19   Christine Tamblyn, 'Significant Others: Social Documentary as Personal Portraiture in Women's Video of the 1980s' in *Illuminating Video: An Essential Guide to Video Art*, D. Hall and S. J. Fifer, (eds)., Aperture, 1992, pp.405–417, p.417.
20   Quoted on http://artievierkant.com/imageobjects.php

SOUTH OF POST-MEDIA

ALEJO DUQUE, FELIPE FONSECA &
OLIVER LERONE SCHULTZ

Transcription by Maria Juliana Yepes Burgos

The first contact between labSurlab and Post-Media Lab developed out of an encounter between Aniara Rodado and Oliver Lerone Schultz in Lüneburg late 2011 – a Colombian speaking in French and a German speaking in English. From this grew several visits along with a conviction, on the part of the Post-Media Lab, that in Latin America a very dense and uniquely critical media culture had taken form. This impression was strengthened by parallel exchanges with Felipe Fonseca and MetaReciclagem – an activist network founded in Brazil in 2002, that began by re-cycling computers for communal use and later developed a more generally deconstructive approach to critical appropriation, opposing consumerism and promoting social change. Several productive encounters, for example at labSurlab 2012 (Quito), Video Vortex (Lüneburg) or the transmediale reSource (Berlin), highlighted the need for an exploration of different regional perspectives on post-media practice – especially in light of the on-the-ground experiences in community media production that emerged in discussion.

Felipe and Alejo – long term collaborators and activators of the Latin American alt_media scene – had already met up in 2008 in Geneva in a discussion about labs at the periphery.[1] Oliver's invitation to pick up on that in the context of the Post-Media Lab was a welcome chance to revisit and develop this ongoing conversation, and to re-trace the lines of what had become of labSurlab and Metareciclagem among others. An online conversation followed, in January 2013, which was later solidified into the text below.

Alejo Duque (Colombia / Switzerland), is one of the seed members of the labSurlab network – a network of independent initiatives combining hacklabs, hackspaces, medialabs and all kinds of South American laboratories and biopolitics groups. As a follow-up to labSurlab 2012, Duque visited the Post-Media Lab on a number of occasions. He is a prolific instigator of participatory arts that aim to build cultural agitation across networks, while focusing on the global 'South'. He has worked on setting up community network projects and non-localised hacklabs while being an active member of networks like Bricolabs, dorkbot-[k.o_lab], Co.Operaciones of which he is also one of the initiators. For more, see: http://mdelibre.co/

Felipe Fonseca (Brazil) is a researcher, media activist and cultural producer with a strong focus on networked collaboration, critical appropriation of information technologies, and free/libre/open knowledge/culture. He was co-founder of a number of community media initiatives such as the MetaReciclagem network (http://rede.metareciclagem.org, 2002), Bricolabs (http://bricolabs.net, 2006), MutGamb (http://mutgamb.org, 2007), Lixo Eletrônico (http://lixoeletronico.org, 2008), Desvio (http://desvio.cc, 2009), Rede//Labs (http://redelabs.org, 2010) and Ubalab (http://ubalab.org, 2010), among others. For more, see: http://efeefe.no-ip.org

Oliver Lerone Schultz is one of the coordinators of Post-Media Lab and researcher at the Centre for Digital Cultures at Leuphana University, where he co-curated Video Vortex #9 and is currently involved as one of the Principal Investigators in the project Making Change within the Common Media Lab. For more, see: http://lerone.net

OLIVER LERONE SCHULTZ: The notion of the post-media age is important within a European context, especially given the break-up of (traditional) mass media – which provides the context for the development of potential new forms of media communications and collectivities.[2] Are these contexts of any relevance to you?

FELIPE FONSECA: I think there are different faces for what could be called the age of mass media. It was radically stronger in our context in developing countries, I think. In Brazil, for instance, 20 years ago, we had one single relevant broadcast company, Rede Globo. It wasn't only TV but a media conglomerate that had newspapers, a big TV channel and radio stations all over the country. It is said they managed then to pressure TV manufacturers to limit the amount of remote controls produced in the country to a maximum of 5 percent of TV sets until around 1990. So we were behind in the way mass media developed when compared to other countries, but at the same time the kind of control and the political presence of mass media was really heavy. I like to think we are in better times now, with more options of information channels, tens of millions accessing the internet and so on. On the other hand, people are getting more superficial. People want to buy, people want to have money, and that's pretty much everything that people aspire to these days.

The idea of post-media makes sense in a way. But I'm not so sure whether the age of mass media can be analysed as a coherent whole, given the wide

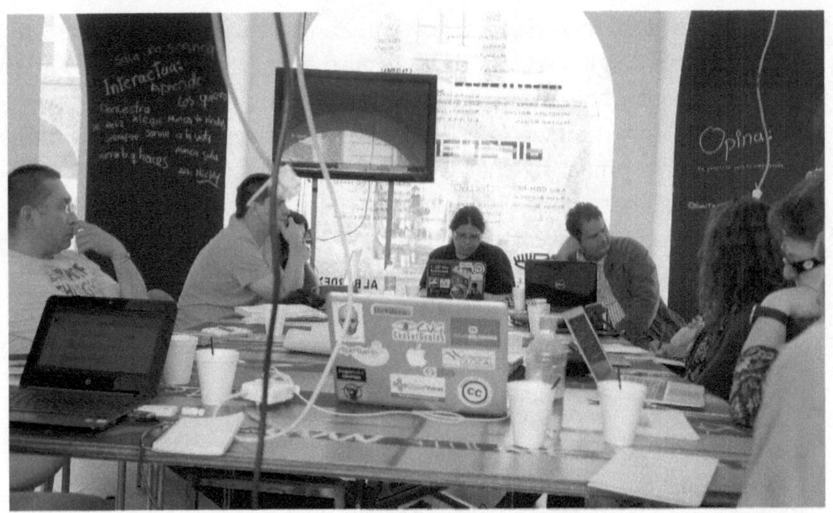

Mesa de Trabajo: Cultura digital y políticas públicas – one of more than two dozen events at the labSurlab 2012 – La Vuelta al Sur. Centro de Arte Contemporaneo, Quito, Ecuador. Photo by Oliver Lerone Schultz

variety of modes it has adopted in different contexts. Thus I'm also not sure that a post-media age is an exact description of the current day.

ALEJO DUQUE: 'We' have never been modern, and if ever, then 'postmodernity' came first. South America is just another complex and heterogeneous continent, every country full of syncopated inequalities where modern historicity crosses a postmodernity of sorts, based on a few centuries old 'mestizaje' at times opaque, at times transparently composed by unintelligible alternate spaces.[3] But for many if not all of those southern communities it is not a question of being 'post' or 'modern'. In the South such notions are somewhat imported, they land real-time within processes of hybridisation-pura.[4] Communities always live in risk, completely unaware of these conceptual and remote classifications of 'prepostmortems'. The 'lack' of any kind of theoretical back ups doesn't stop them from taking actions. They don't 'halt' their procedures or methods for finding ways to survive.[5] One could say they theorise in praxis. The lack of Eurocentric theories won't stop any of them from pushing from the 'undergrounds' to reshape a portion of what, on a wider scale, we could define as 'society'.[6]

FF: Getting back to the post-media context, me and some other people started using the term 'post-digital', but of course in the context of Brazil. There was a lot of institutional rhetoric, from governments and universities in the early 2000s about the 'digital society', 'digital culture' and all that, but very little discussion about what that actually meant. Often it felt like being 'on the internet' was something good in itself. Different groups started to criticise that perspective, proposing that we should go beyond access, beyond the digital as a goal in itself. The kind of thing these projects often do is merely create more users of the corporate internet in a completely homogeneous fashion, and that hides the fact that they can be actual authors of the internet, makers of the internet itself – ultimately challenging the ways people interact in networked environments.

We have some peculiarities – Brazilian cultures usually adopt new technologies in a very eager, sometimes obsessive way. Those of us who access the internet[7] are the people who on average spend most time online in the world.[8] Social networks such as Orkut were already big in Brazil before Facebook gained ground worldwide. So it's not only about giving people access to the internet, but also about changing the perspective and making them not only users but also people who can understand how these technologies could help improve their lives and create new possibilities from that. It's about changing the perspective, with the same kind of equipment, the same people, even, the same resources.

Here in Brazil, as in Colombia I imagine, there was a really quick demographic change during the second half of 20th century with a huge growth of urban populations.[9] There were no opportunities for people in rural areas and smaller villages – everyone wanted to live in big cities, and that meant a lot of traditional knowledge was lost because the sons and grandsons of farmers, fishermen and so on wouldn't want to learn from them, like in Ubatuba where I'm working at the moment. People want to get a 'proper job', maybe in an office and move to a bigger city. But I'm not particularly interested in putting more people in an artificial working environment with a computer and a desk in some office. The idea is trying to understand instead how technologies can create new opportunities for the fishermen, create local opportunities so that they don't need to relocate, to go to big cities to get a city job.[10]

AD: Such tensions trace our current 'contested zones' defining what we should fight for since, indeed, there's a permanent media war going on, while we're enduring the hegemony of colonial practices. There are so many different 'digital divides', those gaps between literate people with access to so called 'new' technologies and disconnected, illiterate people living in marginality. To bridge such gaps there's a trend to 'connect' the world via ITC4D projects and OLPC philanthropism.[11] While now, more than before, it's crucial to find ways to become invisible to overreaching networks that exploit every click. Not only for privacy, but simply because everyone should reclaim the right to opacity.[12]

As to 'post-mediality', I suggest tackling it by going backwards – using methods of media-archaeology to search for different examples found in communities that short-circuit any known standard – while being fully aware that tracing such connections often appears as tropicalism or exoticism to the educated scholar.[13] All we have to do is learn first and foremost from those marginalised communities that have enacted this 'lab-thing-ness' long ago. That may help us better define the notion of post-mediality.

OLS: What notion of 'media' are we talking about in these contexts? You talk a lot about constellations in which it is not about digital networks in the final analysis. When I was talking with different people from labSurlab in Quito, Ecuador, there were a lot of references to different kinds of 'mediation', like the interconnection between 'tecnologías ancestrales', social technologies, politics and biotechnology.

FF: Perhaps more important than the question of any specific medium is, how do people approach those media and appropriate them? In MetaReciclagem, people without a deeper understanding of digital technologies are invited to join in a special relationship. It's more about the value of being together, learning from each other and exchanging experiences.

We've had workshops using only paper and pen, because it's not about computers or wireless networks – what matters is not what specific technology or media we are using, but the sense of opening, sometimes breaking and deconstructing these technologies, these media, these technological mean(ing)s, in order to promote some kind of change. That happens in different formats of exchange: a mailing list, meetings, like the two big meetings of MetaReciclagem where people were invited from all over the country to meet up in a specific place, like we did once in Sao Paulo, once in Bahía and last year in Ubatuba. And there are these other little meetings, simple encounters, of people in a café.

But there's another thing here: 'media' in Portuguese is a singular noun, so when you say 'a mídia' in Portuguese in Brazil you are not talking about the plurality of media because you're talking about one single, massive (abstract) intangible thing. So if you talk about media to people in Brazil, it's very often about corporate media. People who are dealing in 'comunicação comunitária' understand 'media' as big corporate, right wing media related to the old powers of big farmers and big industrial powers. So 'media' has a heavy legacy in Brazil.

OLS: How would you qualify the relevance and impact of Guattarian (and Deleuzian) theories in the Latin American context? Guattari was active in Brazil for a time,[14] some of his writings came out of a Brazilian context,[15] but to what extent were those theories around control society or post-media age really taken up? Have they been taken up or been translated into the discourses relevant to Latin American contexts?[16]

FF: I'm really not comfortable drawing out a single line of thought since there are a number of different, and often very contradictory theories that people are trying to apply to the way things happen in collaborative configurations. There is the Deleuzo-Guattarian influence of course, the description of the society of control, the rhizomes as escape routes, as well as Guattari's direct influence in activist media, especially the Brazilian free radio movement.[17] But on the other hand, there's a big influence of the more concrete tactical media theories.[18] Some people refer to semiotics, others adhere to a more integrated perspective by way of Manuel Castells etc., and within activist networks a number of people don't refer to any kind of academic theory. In and around MetaReciclagem there's a kind of messy environment where discussions touch on a broad set of references, and it's always on the edge of chaos. I wouldn't try to impose a single theoretical framework onto our actions because that consensus was never there.

AD: There are many more social groups (appearing and disappearing) than the number of first world educated academics can study, classify and bring to light. It's sad to see the parameters of study and approach that dominate in Colombian academia completely missing from the 'North-Continental' focus and style of research. Another post-colonial pattern. A case of endocolonisation inside academia.

OLS: Post-Media Lab (PML) has just had a discussion – that included Alejo – about the critical need to 'patch' existing technologies so as to render them functional for communities.[19] There is this notion that under techno-capitalism all technologies – like the net – are in principle always 'broken'.[20]

It sounds like you both, in different ways, are talking a lot about approaches to fix, correct or replace technologies. But on the other hand it seems what is more central to your accounts is a broken social fabric. Felipe, you made the observation that the older generations and communities are 'bleeding out', implying the subsumption of these communities within new modes of valorisation occurring through processes of urbanisation and metropolisation – 'the recomposition, revaluing, and devaluing of local cultures through globalisation'.[21] You also highlight how these traditional knowledges don't just automatically survive through their forms of communalisation.[22] So, how do these dimensions relate to each other, in your view?

FF: First, let me just say that what I suggested before about the fisherman can be (and often is) criticised. While there is this interest in using technologies to help communities, at the other extreme there are people who apply a conservationist take on traditional cultures, in detrimental ways – but I recognise the root of their criticism. For instance, when we started discussing digital culture with the Ministry of Culture, a lot of people would tell us 'You shouldn't put computers in these communities when there is no understanding about how to use these computers...', and in a sense that's excluding people before they even have access. On the other hand, no single technology will solve all the problems of a given community or social group, and more often than not they only change the configuration of issues of power, wealth and safety in a very superficial way.

This tension between respecting traditional social dynamics and promoting the appropriation of new possibilities is rather common. It requires or even induces, as mentioned before, a kind of hybrid culture. There is something about Brazilian cultures – and it can be exaggerated, caricatured – described by the Brazilian modernist movement in the 1920s. Oswald de Andrade suggested in the *Anthropophagic Manifesto* that we acquire culture and knowledge from other cultures, but we mix them, we 'eat' and 'digest' other cultures to create our own. Oswald uses this story of a Portuguese priest, Bispo Sardinha, during colonial times. The story goes that he was eaten by the Caetés people... and that was a kind of way these people had of acquiring the knowledge of their opponents.[23]

I like to see the way new technologies are appropriated in Brazil in a related way. We use mobile phones and social networks almost obsessively. But it's not that we believe all the Californian ideology discourse – that everybody is going to be connected and then we won't need the government, everybody would be better off in small groups, virtual communities self-organised via digital technologies and all that shit. Instead, there is a feeling that we can use those same technologies our way, to do whatever we want to. And that can be easily understood, as we are not in a strategic position with regards to those technologies – meaning, there is very little Brazilian contribution to designing and producing them. But we will – tactically, De Certeau might add – make use of whatever technologies are available to address our particular issues.

OLS: If we bring this general perspective back into the context of what you are doing and engaging in, what does labSurlab or MetaReciclagem embody in terms of approaching or building alternatives, or forming new collectivities and subjectivities in confronting these issues?

AD: Both are very different – labSurlab and MetaReciclagem. The work labSurlab does – as I see it – is to first open the space for representation for marginal groups that never had the chance to share what they are doing.[24] Communities that, as stated before, live in risk. In Colombia to do work in media-activism deserves recognition as a task of the utmost importance; and for labSurlab-Medellín this was pivotal. At the end of the day, what is crucial within the labSurlab network is that we are able to elaborate a common language among some different groups from South American countries. In my experience, and I can't really speak for the whole network/group/collective, labSurlab is reshaping itself every day. One thing was how we were two years ago, when we were in Medellín, another thing is what happened in Quito, at labSurLab #2,[25] and another thing is today, in 2013, when we only operate through IRC channels, a mailing list and a group in the n-1.cc platform.[26] Since there's great need for and interest in the praxis of everyday networks of collaboration some of us have been lead into a project we called Co.Operaciones.[27] So, as to the question, a very small 'yes' regarding 'building new ways', and this process helps us to reshape our society to some degree.

FF: So what is MetaReciclagem? We started around ten years ago as a group of people receiving donated computers, recovering them and installing free and open source software, and passing them on to social projects. We soon realised that we were not together because of computers or even free software itself, but instead for what lies behind the opening, understanding and interfering with technologies. In the course of these ten years, we've changed what we call 'technologies': not only computers and mobile phones

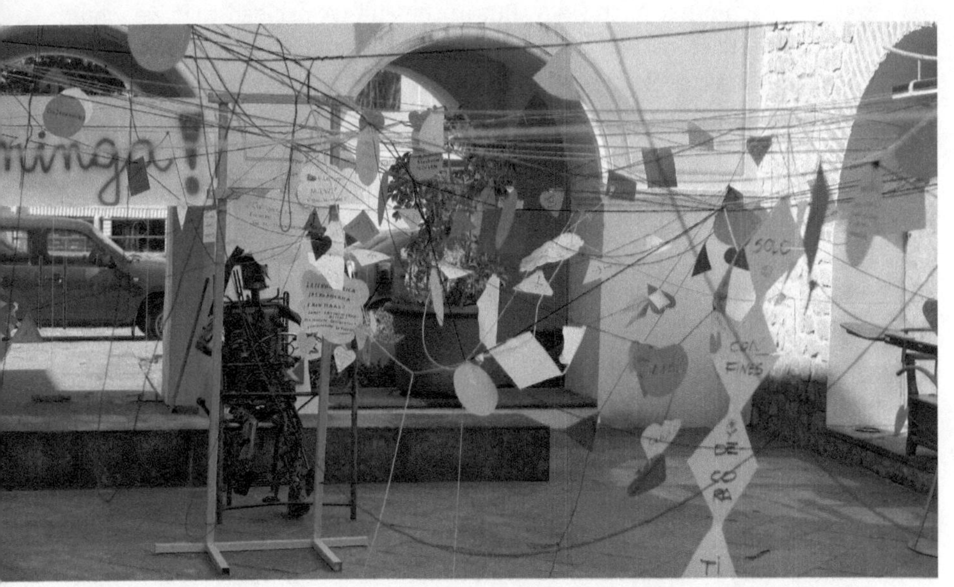

Collective issue and vision mapping for 'Una vuelta al Sur – por la construcción y evolución de maneras de acción colectiva', Centro de Arte Contemporaneo, Quito, Ecuador. Photo by Oliver Lerone Schultz

but also farming, cooking or even organising meetings. We've also changed from saying we were deconstructing technologies to saying we promoted their re-appropriation for a while – and later on called it 'technological appropriation for social change'.

Getting back to the idea of identities and networks, subjectivities and so on, MetaReciclagem has a very particular mode of organising. We had this big discussion ten years ago, one year after we started MetaReciclagem. Some of us were trying to create one institution to represent MetaReciclagem. We had huge fights at that time, and there are still some people who won't speak to each other to this day. But in the end we decided that we would never again try to create a single institution: MetaReciclagem would be a network where people can create their own local arrangements.

There were some singular conditions ten years ago when we started out. It was basically the same time that Lula got elected as president. It was the first time in 40 years that a group linked to the Brazilian left field was the head of the federal government. They had a lot of interesting ideas which had been evolved within the third sector over decades, but didn't have a public staff to implement the politics they wanted and didn't exactly know how to do things.

The idea of digital inclusion emerged like that. It was a commonplace that people were becoming connected around the world but impoverished communities did not have any access. The question then was what to do about it. For concrete solutions, they had to call people from activists groups who were working with alternatives. That's how we got involved with politics in Brazil. It is not that we believed the whole digital inclusion rhetoric, but suddenly there was this open field for experimentation with official support and some resources. And there wasn't any stabilised body of knowledge about these things. We never believed that much in the goals of power, of the government. But these 'outsider' networked contexts did influence the public policies that are currently being implemented, bringing in political issues of free/open licensing, reform of copyright law, respect for traditional cultures and their knowledge, social networking as political organisation, a critical position towards consumerism and the logic of economics.

But it can be said, with all this involvement with different institutions, that some of us were actually invited by the government to implement public policies. Our world view has changed a lot during this time. When we started almost a decade ago, some of us – urban, progressive, internet-savvy activists (myself included, I must confess) – thought we would be going to poor Brazilian neighbourhoods or regions and teaching people how to become fully developed 21st century citizens, based upon a 'totally new' collaborative ethics made possible by digital networking. The truth is that often it was quite the opposite: they were teaching us a lot about simple human values like generosity, sharing, dynamic social formations oriented to problem solving, and so on. We have learnt a lot from the landless workers' movement, the organised hip hop movement and other prominent social movements.

OLS: What do you think are appropriate spaces to enable and systematise these encounters between self-organisation, experimentation and institutional landscapes? In Europe everyone is setting up a 'Lab' these days...

AD: Medellín for example sells itself as a City of Innovation, the 'Most Educated'. To contest this, we just published a book based on some records from labSurlab-Medellín and Co.Operaciones. In it the MIT Lab is not precisely quoted as a role model, it is actually defined as the Military Institute of Technology.[28] The book also invites us to reclaim the traditional form of the minga as a way to operate today, reaching back to learn from the indigenous and extremely underestimated communities.[29]

FF: The idea of a lab is still elastic enough for us to decide to use it to name spaces that host developments that wouldn't take place these days in NGOs, universities or businesses. As the public becomes privatised, as universities are increasingly being evaluated by 'scientific productivity', and companies obviously cannot loose track of profit, a lab can be a place for resistance. This doesn't mean that 'labs' can't be assimilated by the spectacle society. Rio de Janeiro, the ever more hyped city in Brazil – now even worse due to the upcoming Olympics and World Cup – has a lot of 'media labs' being created in which it is all about making money and becoming famous. But at least here the term is under dispute as we speak.

OLS: Both of you sketch an ethos of open and at the same time non-institutionalised networks. In parts of the European context there has been some renewed scepticism, like Jamie King's take on the 'impasse of political organisation', claiming that openness 'is not in and of itself an immediately sufficient alternative to the bankrupt structures of representation.'[30] You implicitly sketch a problematisation of certain forms of representation that seems to resemble what in Deleuzo-Guattarian terminology can be dubbed 'micro-politics'. So if you consider the pragmatics of political positioning, what are the principles and values that connect to your activities, or that connect these loose, heterogeneous groupings?

FF: There's always this discussion about how to organise networks in order to reflect what has been created in the network. Ned Rossiter and Geert Lovink wrote about 'organised networks', for instance.[31] In MetaReciclagem we decided to stay one step ahead of that, I guess. So the network can never be, what Jamie King calls 'constituted'.[32] MetaReciclagem is pre-constituted, always changing, being challenged and reinventing itself. We only need to learn to deal with that.

Whenever I establish a partnership, I can refer to MetaReciclagem but I can't attribute that partnership to it. Nobody would be able to make a partnership with MetaReciclagem itself because MetaReciclagem does not exist in the world of formal partnerships, but you could as a member create a simple arrangement there that would be related to the network as long as s/he follows some principles: using free and open technologies; documenting everything in our autonomous digital infrastructure – basically a mailing list and a wiki; and working towards the promotion of social change for more collaborative, equal and sustainable futures. That led to the emergence of a lot of different institutional arrangements, so there are people who have partnerships with schools or with municipalities or even companies, or people who set up their own small consultancy businesses. But none of them can speak in the name of MetaReciclagem. MetaReciclagem does not have a coherent 'self'; so it doesn't matter if some of us have arrangements with, say, the public power in one locality and others criticise the same arrangements.

At the same time some partnerships will always rely on representation because that's the only way some institutions are able to operate, for reasons of accountability or whatnot. If you're talking about a public school, they need someone to refer to, someone to contact, someone to complain to if things don't work out as they should. But something that emerged in our discussions in Brazil is the recognition that there are some contexts which require representation, whilst remaining sceptical about what that implies. We are talking about the self-sabotage of leaderships. We don't want the golden dream of having a rich, problem-solving institution. There is a good amount of money being made with MetaReciclagem projects, while I still can't pay my personal debts. And that doesn't bother me. So there's this kind of thing. A lot of people could have a prominent role in MetaReciclagem but decide not to – not to become that sort of person. We always try to remain open and curious about new things and new people. In a weird way, that allows us to influence politics in a different way.

All this may sound obvious these days, but professional activists used to say we were wrong. I even heard once: 'you have to become an institution, otherwise you won't have any impact in political decisions'. And this is definitely not true.[33] By acting in a truly distributed fashion, MetaReciclagem members managed to influence a number of public projects and policies. There is no consensus about what MetaReciclagem is, but one of its most used definitions is as an open methodology that anyone can use.

AD: All we have done, both with labSurlab and Co.Operaciones, is suggest what in Brazil is proposed by undertakings like Redelabs, among others.[34] It is fundamental for us to be able to go forward into a common reading and conversation (like the current one) with peers from other countries.

Last year (2012) in Medellín – because of some 'innovation' funding – what we decided to do was to get more into developing actions and activities on the ground. Instead of producing more talks, we thought, let's do things, let's do actions. But, we thought, let's do it in a way that's horizontal as much as we can manage. So we invited a varied individuals and initiatives like Platohedro, alongside institutions.[35] So we got the resources to organise workshops in the neighbourhoods alongside supporting a group of people from Medellín to be able to get to Quito and participate in the labSurlab meeting. For Co.Operaciones we didn't have a specific location or space, so we embraced our permanent nomadic status, that after all gives us some tactical strength, and we made the workshops in many different places within the city, casting a wider map than the localised event, fixed to only one point.[36] It was complex.

OLS: You yourselves drift between Latin American, European and other contexts – does the diasporic enter into the equations of what you are doing?[37]

FF: LabSurlab, which to me is a kind of movement with great potential, was first envisioned in Europe. But it doesn't matter that the first meeting that eventually gave rise to it happened in Europe. Its focus was a Latin American perspective, and the exact location of its inception is irrelevant, in the end. But I think that the sense of precarity is always there, in different forms – including here the very chance to meet at Interactivos?10.[38] A lot of people from Latin-America met in Madrid because we couldn't afford to meet in

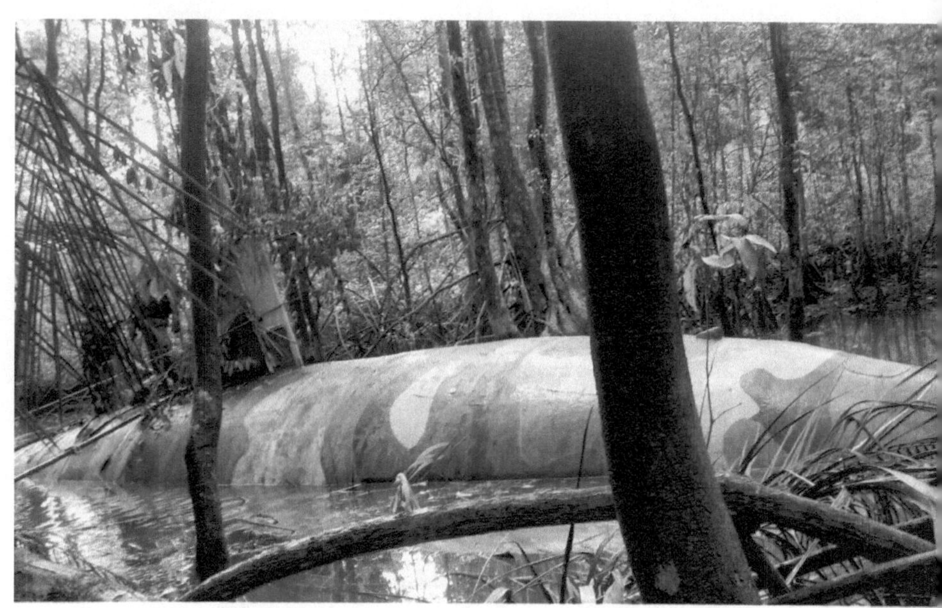

A fully-operational submarine built for the primary purpose of transporting multi-ton quantities of cocaine located near a tributary close to the Ecuador/Colombia border that was seized by the Ecuador Anti-Narcotics Police Forces and Ecuador Military authorities with the assistance of the DEA.
Photo by US Drug Enforcement Administration – 2 July 2010

South America. And that was a very interesting moment because there were more than 20 people from different Latin American countries; something that wouldn't happen often in Latin America.

AD: I can tell how that happened, we were all together in Spain during interactivos?10 organised by the Medialab-Prado.[39] There was also a parallel meeting called LABtoLAB.[40] We were invited to join in with their discussions. One of their central discussion points was the notion of precarity. For us coming from the South, there was this contradiction of Europe being such a rich place – the place smelt of BBQ.[41] Indeed the so called financial crisis had hit the cultural initiatives in Spain and elsewhere, but when there are millions of people striving to survive that's the kind of precarity I'm wary about. I couldn't talk about it while we had access to food and beers, there was even someone cooking for us. For me precarity, fuck, is never having had a chance to make a meeting in a stable place, to host chats over IRC or mailing lists – even those are spaces for the 'rich'. At the meeting some of the Latin American participants decided to create a network to solve specific issues related to the Centros de Cultura de España in Latin America. Since neither Alejandro Araque nor me belonged to any of those institutions, that same night we decided to start a group at the n-1 network called labSurlab.[42] It was a reaction to what orbited there at LABtoLAB.

'Diaspora' is a term that I don't want to use too much, but that relates to a search. And I say that because I like to think in terms of the Caribbean space.[43] Basically all our 'connections' with, say, Brazil can be better bridged not through the anti-colonialist or essentialist search for a lost surrealist Otherness, but through a search for the particular differences that can put us into relation. So, it might be easier for me and my friends to relate to each other across different cultures, even if we don't come from the same path, but it is certain that in music, food and survival skills we share enough.

OLS: If we are looking at these 'wild' processes, which are subsumed, or whose subsumption is threatened by the kind of media capitalism you are talking about – then, what about rephrasing all these issues into questions of alternative forms of valorisation, and through this to questions of value production/extraction or exploitation?[44] When Nestor Garcia Canclini speaks of 'the digitalisation and mediation of rural processes of production, circulation, and consumption, which transfers the initiative and economic and cultural control to transnational corporations', you seem to be looking for ways to steer clear of that.[45] But what are these new assemblages or these networked communities etc., actually gravitating towards, in terms of alternative systems of value-production, value in a non-economical sense. What is positively producing coherence in programmatics, ethos or values?[46]

FF: I don't think we can stay away or afford to totally refuse any kind of assimilation or exploitation. But also we shouldn't play a passive role by believing the discourse. We can accept exploitation sometimes. But we won't stay in that position more than necessary.

AD: I think that our most precious value is the affective network we build outside commercial sponsoring. When Felipe was talking about the funding they got, which could even be put to experiment and result in a change of governmental policies, I can't help but compare this with Colombia where we have never seen something like this. The people in charge here obey the Telefonica mentality where technology, in the end, means market reach. For example in Medellin, Colombia, Bill Gates, the MIT Lab and Mark Zuckerberg are equivalent to Hollywood's greatest heroes, and entrepreneurial role models at the same time. What can you expect from the director of a public initiative when s/he is all about the new iPad and other similar gadgets?

The Brazilian case seems in a way similar to when George Soros gave funding to the young people in the Balkans and the Baltic for cultural projects. This was the origin of Re-Lab, nowadays RIXC, and so many other groups and artists that had paved the paths of what network collaborations and art can be about.[47] I actually think that these examples relate better to us in the South than those happening in the centre of Europe or the USA. Why? Because they are at the periphery, because they don't speak the same language, because they have been colonies for decades, because they lived at risk and know what precarity means.

FF: Coming back to the question, whether there is a common characteristic between the diversity of projects and actions in MetaReciclagem and similar networks, it could be an attempt to oppose and resist the trend in society to have a single frame of reference. In a way that is this idea that everything can be translated into numbers, everything can be quantified and everything should be productive.

MetaReciclagem was a kind of process through which we, from our urban, academic, contemporary perspectives, learnt that things are deeper. There are places in Brazil where you may feel as though you are in the 19th century, places where you can order someone's death for a couple reais, or you will only have water to drink after walking 15 kilometres. All these material spaces are contemporary all at once. We cannot substitute all that for a single rhetoric in which MetaReciclagem would become a slice of reality and define itself strategically in the global scenario. We are always deconstructing people who are too sure of themselves. Common sense tells us that there are plenty of alternatives to whatever we believe. To every agnostic activist there is someone advocating ancestral spirituality, to every free software enthusiast there is a technophobe. A big diversity of opinions, fields of knowledge, expectations, positions in any given subject exist – that sometimes can be very tiresome, because anything you say will be criticised. But people keep insisting.

AD: We definitely need to learn more from those existing communities that are there with their knowledge and know-how. And in the case of Colombia these are often considered 'illegal' networks which, of course, depends on the morality that classifies them. We are talking here about people that have to find a way to survive, and many criminal activities are just default in their context as a consequence also of global economic pressure. It is nothing less than a desperate act that is expressed by a DIY narco-submarine, built in the middle of the country thousands of kilometres from the sea.[48] It involves huge violence to see people getting into them to cross part of the Atlantic for the sake of enabling some party time in the North. It's similar to the cars that are being reused by the Cubans to try to escape the island. So if there's something to learn, it's that we need to try to pause and turn back to listen, like in the case of the *minga*. We have all these possibilities in the remaining ancestral communities, which are at the same time disappearing every day with their languages and knowledge, while we're NOT learning anything from them! That's why we need to push pause and stop. And that's where 'digital divides' and gaps might actually need to stay in place.

Footnotes

1   See: http://archive.org/details/ElLabEsLaRed
2   See, Félix Guattari, 'Remaking Social Practices', Gary Genosko, *The Guattari Reader*, 1996, Oxford et.al.: Blackford, pp.262-272; Compare with Michael Goddard, 'Félix and Alice in Wonderland: The Encounter Between Guattari and Berardi and the Post-Media Era', in this volume, p.44.
3   Anjali Prabhu, 'Interrogating Hybridity', *Diacritics*, Vol. 35, No.2., Summer, 2005;

Nestor Garcia Canclini, *Culturas híbridas: Estrategias para entrar y salir de la modernidad*, 1990, México: Grijalbo.

4   'The word hybridisation seems more ductile for the purpose of naming not only the mixing of ethnic or religious elements but the products of advanced technologies and modern or postmodern social processes.' Néstor García Canclini, *Hybrid Cultures: Strategies for Entering and Leaving Modernity*, 2005, Minneapolis: University of Minnesota Press, p.xxxiv.

5   'It is useful to warn against the overly pleasant versions of mestizaje. That is why it is best to insist that the object of study is not hybridity, but the processes of hybridization.' Ibid., p.xxi.

6   'In this context one might think of 'savage hybridity' to point out that the condition of unspeakability among a range of identitarian positions, typical of contemporary societies, 'ungrounds' both hegemonic and subaltern social groups.' Ibid.

7   Estimated to be 94 million people in December 2012, http://info.abril.com.br/noticias/internet/brasil-atinge-94-2-milhoes-de-pessoas-conectadas-14122012-32.shl

8   An estimated 69 hours a month in 2011, http://info.abril.com.br/noticias/internet/brasil-atinge-94-2-milhoes-de-pessoas-conectadas-14122012-32.shl

9   '[...] there seems to be something different going on here, even more than just the qualitative shift that comes with the quantitative rapidity and mass of urban growth that has Mexico City or Sao Paulo experiencing in just one generation what London went through in ten and Chicago in three.' David Harvey, *Possible Urban Worlds*, 2000, Amersfoort: Twynstra Gudde Management Consultants, p.16.

10   'The theory of hybridization should take into account the movements that reject it. Such movements do not only arise from fundamentalisms that oppose religious syncretism and cross-cultural mestizaje. There is resistance to the acceptance of these and other forms of hybridization because such phenomena generate insecurity among different cultural groups and conspire against their ethnocentric self-esteem.' Nestor Garcia Canclini, op. cit., xxxvii.

11   ICT4D: Information and communication technologies for development; OLPC: 'One Labtop per Child', a campaign supported by Nicholas Negroponte, funder of the MIT Media Lab. In one TED-talk you can see a video where Negroponte comes to Colombia to give away laptops to a remote and small little town. He lands in a BlackHawk Helicopter, very proud that the Colombian army is handing over these plastic wrapped devices. See: http://www.ted.com/talks/nicholas_negroponte_takes_olpc_to_colombia.html

12   'Édouard Glissant – Wikipedia, the free encyclopedia', 2005, http://en.wikipedia.org/wiki/%C3%89douard_Glissant

13   Siegfried Zielinski and Gloria Custance, *Deep Time of the Media: Toward an Archaeology of Hearing and Seeing by Technical Means*, Cambridge, MA: MIT Press, 2006.

14   'In the early 1980s, at the end of two decades of military dictatorship, Félix Guattari travelled to Brazil on the invitation of fellow psychoanalyst and cultural critic, Suely Rolnik, [....] They organised a series of meetings, interviews and talks across the country, debating those changes with people who were directly engaged in producing them. Some of these were edited and reworked by Rolnik into a book, *Molecular Revolution in Brazil*, Rodrigo Nunes and Ben Trott, '"There is no scope for futurology; history will decide": Félix Guattari on molecular revolution', *Turbulence* #4, 2008.

15   Félix Guattari and Suely Rolnik, *Molecular Revolution in Brazil*, 1986, New York:
     Semiotext(e), 2008. Trans. of *Micropolitica: Cartografias do Desejo*. See also, Gary
     Genosko, *The Party without Bosses: Lessons On Anti-Capitalism From Guattari and
     Lula*, Semaphore series, Arbeiter Ring, 2003.
16   Here also thinking of manifestos from the context of Latin American political poetics
     of resistance like: Ricardo Dominguez, 'Post-Media Impossibilities (Part One) Or
     Mayan Technologies For The People', 1999, c-theory, e081.
17   Arlindo Machado, Caio Magri and Marcelo Masagao, *Radios Livres: A Reforma
     Agraria No Ar*, Sao Paulo: Editora Brasiliense S.A., 1986.
18   See also, Clemens Apprich, 'Remaking Media Practices – From Tactical Media to
     Post-Media' in this volume, p.122.
19   'Networks out of Hands' roundtable with Christopher Kullenberg/Stephan Urbach
     from Telecomix, Rena Tangens from FoeBuD, Lonneke van der Velden/Daniel Reusche
     via Unlike Us, Alejo Duque from labSurlab and Oliver Lerone Schultz from PML.
     Part of 'reSource 002: Out of Place, Out of Time', Kunstraum Bethanien, Berlin, 22–
     24 August, 2012. See postmedialab.org and http://www.academia.edu/2123974/
     Networks_out_of_Hands_-_Patching_the_Internet.
20   See also Alexander R. Galloway and Eugene Thacker, *The Exploit: A Theory of
     Networks*, 2007, Minneapolis: University of Minnesota Press.
21   Nestor Garcia Canclini, op. cit., p.xi; see also, Li T Murray, 'Capitalism, Indigeneity
     and the Management of Dispossession', *Current Anthropology* 51(3), 2010, pp.385–
     414.
22   See: Ton Salman, Anke van Dam and Rik Hoekstra : The legacy of the disinherited :
     popular culture in Latin America: modernity, globalization, hybridity and authenticity,
     1996, Amsterdam: Centrum voor Studie en Documentatie van Latijns Amerika
     (CEDLA).
23   Supposedly the Caetés had a tradition by which, during a war between different
     tribes, once the first man had died his tribe was defeated, and the body of the dead
     warrior would be eaten by his enemies. But the deceased was considered to be the
     bravest of all. By eating his body, his opponents would acquire all his courage, his
     spirits, his knowledge.
24   'ORGANIZACION SUR DEL CIELO (SanLuis Km5 – Via la calera ...', 2010, http://
     vimeo.com/9500219; 'La Direkta – Colombia [#labSurlab] – YouTube.' 2011. http://
     www.youtube.com/watch?v=TQ7_4E5nH8Q; 'Antena Mutante', 2008, http://www.
     antenamutante.net/ ... and others.
25   'La Vuelta al Sur', 15-23 June 2012. The website for labSurlab #2 at Quito is
     https://quito.labsurlab.org/. For a Prezi presentation on the issues and topics of
     labSurlab #2 by Camilo Cantor see, http://prezi.com/e6epodocoxj4/labsurlab-quito/
26   N-1: labSurlab, 2012, https://n-1.cc/g/labsurlab
27   Co.Operaciones, 2012, http://cooperaciones.mdelibre.co/
28   'Speakers at MIT's annual tri-service Presidential Pass-in-Review, held April 28 on
     Briggs Field, touched on the strength of military tradition at MIT, from early radar
     work to the current ROTC program.' Sarah H. Wright, News Office,'Event honors MIT
     military tradition', *MIT News*, 5 May 1999, http://web.mit.edu/newsoffice/1999/rotc-
     0505.html. A version of this article appeared in the 5 May, 1999 issue of MIT Tech
     Talk Volume 43, Number 29.
29   This describes a collective effort whereby every individual commits resources and
     time to achieve a common objective: '"Minga" is a Quechua word meaning "collective

work" with wide currency among popular and poor sectors, both indigenous and mestizo, of the Andean republics… By calling their movement a minga, the indigenous participants call attention to both the work that must go into politics and the idea that that work must be collective. They also, of course, reclaim it from long histories of state-led attempts to organise and control collective politics and community organisation.' Deborah Poole, 'The Minga of Resistance: Policy Making From Below', NACLA.org, Feb 16 2009. See also, http://ia601504.us.archive.org/29/items/labSurlab-Co.Operaciones/LabsurlabCoOperaciones.pdf

30 Jamie King, 'The Packet Gang', 2004, *Mute* Vol. 1, No. 27. http://www.metamute.org/editorial/articles/packet-gang.

31 Geert Lovink and Ned Rossiter, *Organized Networks: Media Theory, Creative Labour, New Institutions*, 2006, Rotterdam: NAi Publishers and the Institute of Network Cultures. On the 'Will to Network' see also Geert Lovink, (ed.), *From Weak Ties to Organized Networks, Ideas, Reports, Critiques*, Amsterdam: Institute of Network Cultures, 2009.

32 Jamie King, 'On the Plane of the Para-Constituted: Towards a Grammar of Gangpower' http://www.shiftspace.cc/jamie/gang_grammar.pdf

33 For a thorough discussion of this issue see, *Instituent Practices*, Transversal, EIPCP, 2007, http://eipcp.net/transversal/0707 and *Instituent Practices II*, Transversal, EIPCP, 2007, http://eipcp.net/transversal/0507

34 http://redelabs.org/

35 http://platohedro.blogspot.com/

36 http://cooperaciones.mdelibre.co/?talleres

37 For a cultural-political reading of the productive figure of the diaspora and particular perspectives connected to it, see Nicholas Mirzoeff, 'The Multiple Viewpoint: Diaspora and Visual Culture' In Nicholas Mirzoeff (ed.), *The Visual Culture Reader*, London/New York: Routledge, 2002, pp.204–214. For a more socio-political reading and links to the current crisis of the concept of national citizenship and alternative 'spaces' of the civil see, Saskia Sassen, 'Global Cities and Diasporic Networks: Microsites in Global Civil Society', Helmut Anheier et. al., *Global Civil Society*, 2002, Oxford: Oxford University Press, pp.217–238, or http://transnationalism.uchicago.edu/Diasporic Network.pdf.

38 http://medialab-prado.es/article/taller-seminario_interactivos10_ciencia_de_barrio

39 http://medialab-prado.es/

40 LABtoLAB, 2009, http://www.labtolab.org/

41 For a current take on this tension in perspective see: Michael Burawoy and Karl von Holdt (2012): 'Precarity from the South', http://www.swopinstitute.org.za/files/PRECARITY_FROM_THE_SOUTH_overview.pdf

42 N-1: labSurlab, https://n-1.cc/g/labsurlab

43 Norman Girvan, 'Martinique is not a Polynesian Island', 2011, http://www.normangirvan.info/wp-content/uploads/2011/02/dash-into-to-discurso-antillano.pdf

44 See also 'A Glossary of Subsumption' at The Public School in Berlin on 23–25 January; see: http://www.postmedialab.org/glossary-subsumption-workshop.

45 Nestor Garcia Canclini, 2005, op. cit., p.xxxix.

46 For a link between the concept of coherence and subjectivity compare: 'Information cannot be reduced to its objective manifestations; it is, essentially, the production of subjectivity, the becoming-consistent [prise de consistance] of incorporeal universes.' – Felix Guattari, 'Remaking Social Practices', op. cit., p.266.

47   http://rixc.lv/

48   'Drug smugglers will resort to any number of creative DIY solutions for bringing
      their illicit goods to the United States, from marijuana catapults to mega-tunnels.
      But a new fleet of diesel-powered, fully submersible narco-subs could be the bane
      of law enforcement's existence [...] The subs are built in the thick jungles of central
      America, where they would be hard to detect via aerial surveillance.' Rebecca Boyle,
      'The Next Generation of Cocaine-Smuggling Drug Submarines', POPSCI, 9.11.2012,
      http://www.popsci.com/technology/article/2012-09/new-fleet-impressively-
      seaworthy-drug-submarines-shipping-cocaine-caribbean-0

ACTIVISM AND SCHIZOANALYSIS: THE ARTICULATION OF POLITICAL SPEECH

BRIAN HOLMES

Every way in is a way out.
  – Öyvind Fahlström

Let's start by defining things very simply. An *event* is a break in a normalised flow of experience. When you have to ask what's happening, and why and whether it's dangerous or exciting, or if it means something to you, then your day has been *eventful*. Events can be collective, and they can occur at different scales: urban, national, global. Deliberately breaking the normalised flow of collective experience, with the intent to provoke political debate and action, is what I call *eventwork*.[1]

It's clear this doesn't happen in a vacuum. The generation, communication, interpretation and historicisation of events is a burning issue in control societies where our body rhythms and affective tones are increasingly impacted by so-called crises: urban disasters, financial collapses, crimes, terrorism, wars, etc. Events are typically portrayed on the TV screen as natural phenomena or accidents of fate; but they are intensively worked over by competing fractions of the dominant media, in order to shape the public's reactions and hold them within the limits of normalcy. Since crisis-events occur quite frequently – and are sometimes deliberately manufactured – there are more or less regular patterns of response, whose reiteration lends political life its droning continuity. Take a recent example: the financial crisis of 2008 unleashed astoundingly little protest at the outset, even when cause for outrage was in plain view. Instead, the usual disaster scenario took over: a crescendo of short-term reporting, a longer sequence of legislative posturing, a conditioned habituation to new levels of hypocrisy and abject greed, and a rapid return to speculation and profit-seeking. At the epicentre of the crisis in the United States, it was a full three years before grassroots activists were able to raise any popular resistance. They did so through the deliberately experimental production of a complex, multilayered, open-ended event: the Occupy movement. In the wake of that movement and in the expectation of others, I think we should devote more attention to the most effective form of political intervention currently known on the left. The production of events is the pre-eminent use of that grab-bag of artistic and agitational techniques known as tactical media.[2] Besides, making your own events is a lot more entertaining than what the US military, in its inimitable way, has called 'enduring freedom'.

In this text I'll explore the distributed politics of eventwork, via an analytic cut-up into four distinct and intersecting dimensions: territorial, organisational, theoretical and aesthetic. The scissors for this operation

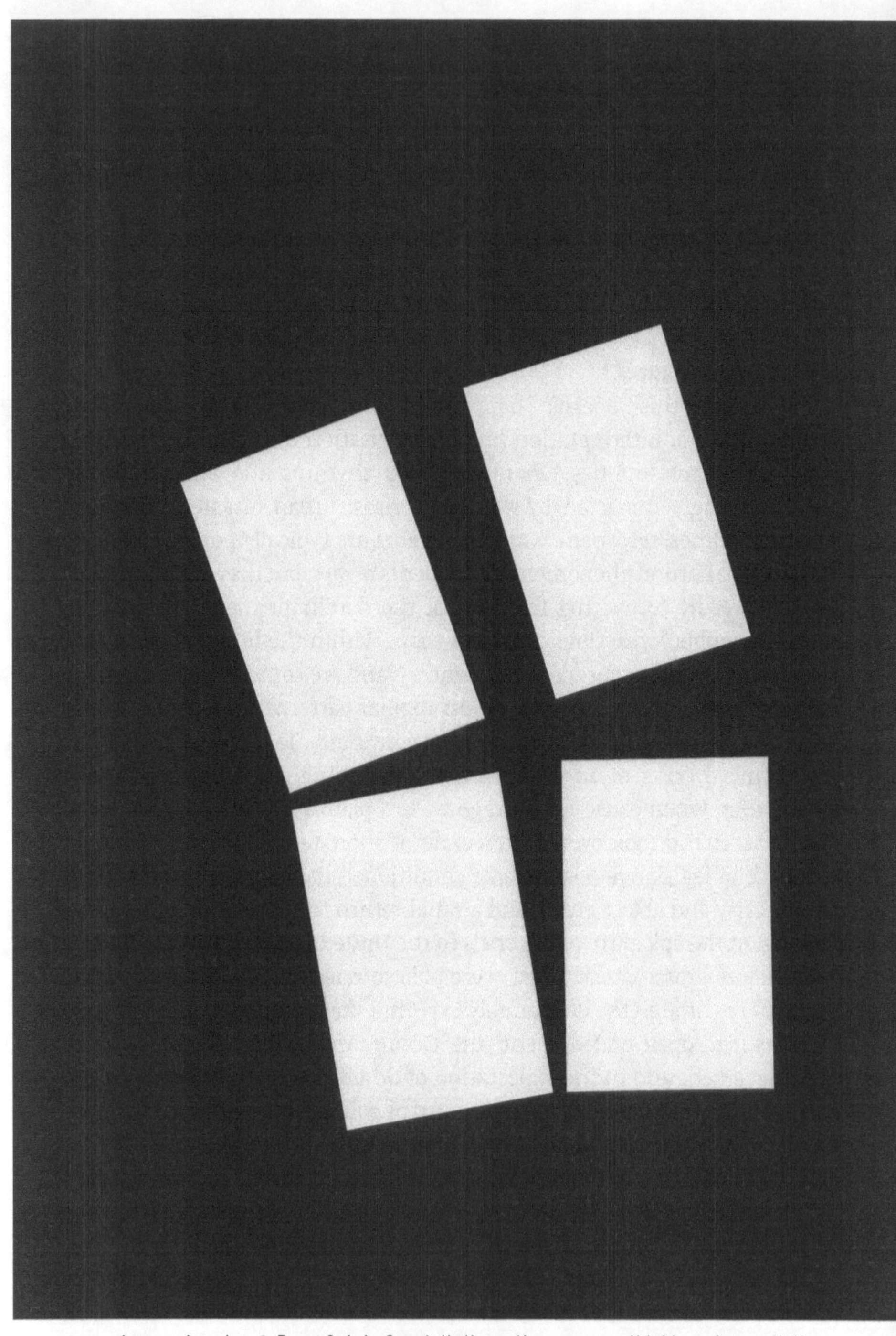

Ayreen Anastas & Rene Gabri, *Constellations: Here we are thinking of an artistic image*, 2013

have been borrowed from the post-structuralist writer, therapist and activist Félix Guattari, and particularly from his strange and hermetic book, only recently translated into English, *Schizoanalytic Cartographies*.[3] To suggest how the concepts of this book might be used in the future, I will also look back at some of the problems to which they responded in the past. What I will *not* do is tell you 'what Guattari really thought' – either about schizoanalysis or the event. In my view, the only way to remain faithful to a practice like his is to appropriate it and thoroughly transform it.

Programmed Societies

If contemporary social life has a *structure*, which appears as an all encompassing destiny, it is because this structure is imposed by organisations with the power to manipulate the reception of events, particularly but not only through the mass media. In the United States, this power was consolidated through the institutional and informational systems that emerged from World War II, from focus groups to the 'world modelling' of J.W. Forrester.[4] Indeed, the imposition of those systems on the country itself and on the rest of the planet constituted the essential 'victory' of the war. The basic principle is that of feedback control loops, whose construction follows a definite order:

1. Gather information about how a population reacts to a wide range of environmental inputs.
2. Construct a mathematical model of the 'system' constituted by the population and its environment.
3. Inject new elements into the real environment on the basis of hypotheses about the mathematical model.
4. Gather fresh information about the results – then adjust all previous steps accordingly.

The general idea here (remember that we are supposed to be living in democracies!) is to manipulate not the individual players, but the rules of the game. A corporation can use these feedback techniques to sell its products, and a government, to support its policies. The history of popular contestation since WWII is that of more-or-less confused, more-or-less conscious reactions to the installation and gradual evolution of structuralising feedback systems.

In a lecture delivered at Documenta 13 in Kassel, Germany, the critical theorist Bruno Bosteels describes postwar French structuralism as a response to the rise of systems theory and cybernetics, which apply mathematical formalisms to human behaviour That might seem a bit strange: because structuralism, with its emphasis on the primary importance of linguistic coding, appears to do exactly the same. However, Bosteels remarks that the leading exponents of structuralism always focused not only on structure as a patterned regularity (and therefore as a determinant cause of behaviour) but also on the way in which the every totalising structure 'seems to harbour within itself a form of inner excess that it cannot control.'[5] The result of structuralist activity was therefore to bring code-based systems up to and beyond their limits, in a movement of traversal and overflow. The drive toward excess was clearly political. As the philosopher Étienne Balibar writes, in a text referenced by Bosteels, 'it was impossible to formulate conditions for *entering* the field of structural or structuralist discourse without immediately looking for the *way out*.'[6]

This paradoxical tendency within the disciplines of structuralism became the predominant concern of the post-structuralists after the 'events' of 1968, which shook both philosophy and society to the core. People began massively looking for a *way out*. Sociologists of the time, such as Alain Touraine, spoke of the '68 movements as a refusal of 'the programmed society'. As Touraine explains, 'All the domains of social life – education, consumption, information, etc. – are being more and more integrated into what used to be called production factors.'[7] That was the leading idea of Keynesian economics: the population's effective demand is the key to the expansion of production. In other words, consumer desire is the feedback loop of industry, and the agenda of capitalism is to structuralise your most intimate existence.

The disruptive events of the '60s can be read as social equivalents of the philosophical search for what makes the structure break down, for its perverse principle of dysfunction, its wild propensity to *self-subversion*. To seek this breakdown in socially generated events whose authors and causes are multiple and to some extent always enigmatic, is not to reinstate any privileged agent who could occupy a position of strategic remove and mastery. It is, instead, to focus on social multiplicity as an   indeterminate potential. The great attraction to tactics over strategy – and therefore, to what is now called 'tactical media' – has it origins here.[8] And these destructuralising events had their consequences in the lives of millions of people, not only in France but across the earth. In scattered sites all over the globe, '68 was the theatre of an audacious but failed revolution. After it was all over the participants must surely have asked themselves: What pushed us to act as we did? What potentials did we reveal? What traps did we fall into? And how could we go further – when what's done in the streets is done?

The radical left movements that re-emerged in the '90s sought explicitly to go beyond the impasses of the '60s and '70s. A totalising ideology (classical Marxism-Leninism) was one such dead-end. A withdrawal to archaic social relations (hippie communalism) was another. The coming revolution would have to be protean, multiform – a *molecular revolution*, in Guattari's words. The arrival of network technologies offered a glimmer of new expressive and cooperative possibilities, the dawn of a post-media era. As he wrote in 1989, in *Schizoanalytic Cartographies*:

> The emergence of these new practices of subjectification of a post-media era will be greatly facilitated by a concerted reappropriation of information and communication technologies in so far as they will increasingly authorize:

> 1. the promotion of innovative forms of consultation and collective action, and in the long run, a reinvention of democracy;
> 2. the miniaturization and personalization of apparatuses, a resingularization of mediatized means of expression. One may assume, in this respect, that it is the extension into a network of databanks that will have the biggest surprises in store for us;
> 3. the multiplication to infinity of 'existential shifters' permitting access to creative mutant Universes.[9]

In short, Guattari believed that the equation 'media = passivity' was on the way out. Yet the experience of the programmed society led many to realise in his wake that the upcoming struggles would also have to face new and increasingly sophisticated techniques for channelling expression, neutralising events and stifling what Michel de Certeau, in the aftermath of '68, had called 'the taking of speech.'[10] Of course De Certeau's phrase cuts both ways, and today there is no more double-edged technology than the internet. The messianic promise of the net was pushed hard by industry, less so by activists and artists. Indeed, much of tactical media is a sophisticated critical and satirical discourse aimed at deflating what a group like Critical Art Ensemble has called the 'promissory rhetoric of technology', while revealing the hidden agendas of corporate and governmental power. Once again it is a matter of *self-subversion*: entering the structure to derail it.

This whole discussion is pointing toward something like a counter-programme. And maybe it's bigger, more self-conscious than you think. Let's put on Guattari's glasses and look not only at the exploits of tactical media, but at the ways they are rooted in existential territories, etherealised in aesthetic rhythms, engaged in self-organised social movements and dissolved into acid critique. Let's try to map out the main vectors of eventwork.

Four Ways In

Guattari's approach to analysis tries to help open up 'collective assemblages of enunciation', or possibilities for taking speech. This does not just mean speaking in the restricted sense: it could be gestures, affects, symbols, practices. The point is to articulate something singular, not systematised, not overcoded in advance. And the point is to articulate it collectively, in public. But the strange thing is that Guattari approaches the collective assemblages through a *schiz*, that is to say, a splitting, a dissociation. Schizoanalysis splits subjectivity into four incommensurable dimensions: Territories, Universes, Phyla and Flows. They are separate and more-or-less autonomous assemblages, even within the experience of a single individual. They are not *functions* of any primary cause or mobilising energy; but they can be approached as *functors*, that is to say, operators of a relational process. Life does not necessarily add up, but we all move through it anyway. Here goes:

1. *Existential Territories.* They are literally grounds, inhabited spaces of the body, pacings, ranges, graspings, sinkholes and sometimes dead ends. Think of a landscape, an ocean, a neighbourhood, a street corner, the four walls of your ecstatic and unbearable room. Territory is not only a category of human settlement but also of ethology, it is the home and at the same time the nest, the lair or the den, the warm and familiar haunt that can coax you into well being or veer off into obsessional repetition: the clamminess of sweat, the black hole of anxiety. It is crucial to realise that in Guattari's fourfold matrix, the Territories lie at the intersection of the real and the virtual, so they can be expressed as the Territories of the Virtually Real. Through their virtuality they relate (or not) to something else:

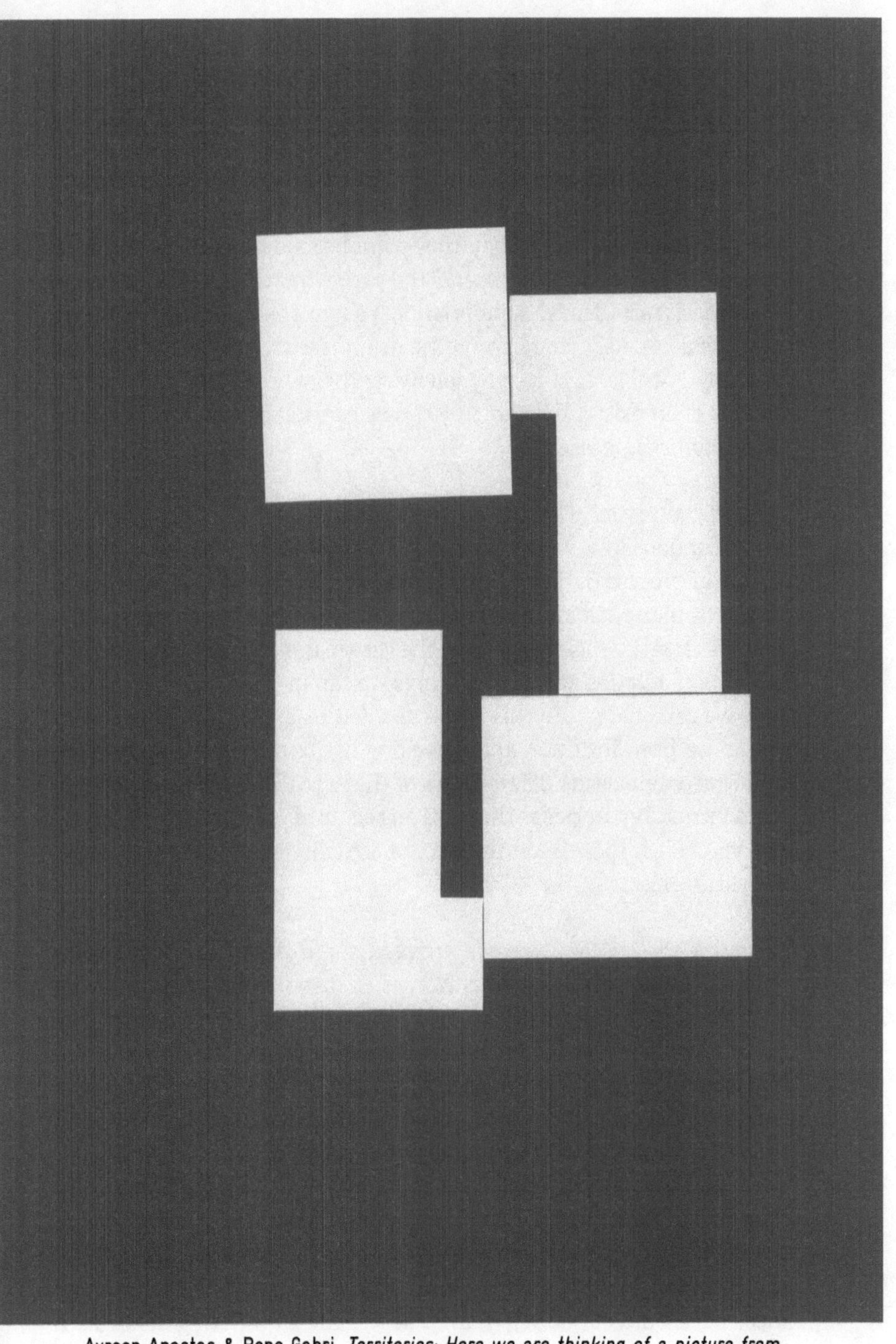

Ayreen Anastas & Rene Gabri, *Territories: Here we are thinking of a picture from 16 Beaver Space*, 2013

2. *Incorporeal Universes of Reference (or of Value).* Now we're talking about the insistence of rhythms, forms, images, aesthetic patterns of all sorts, fragments of poetry or film that return in memory as what Guattari called 'refrains'. It's not the painting on the wall, but the one you see in the dark that matters here. These constellations of Universes are never complete, they are in but not of the body, they point beyond themselves to further horizons. Yet they are what sparks the pathic trance of self-reference, or 'autopoiesis': an affective appropriation, a singularising process that turns the outside in. Reaching beyond the real, these are the Universes of the Virtually Possible. And it is by following their incorporeal call that the bounds of an existential Territory can be overstepped, so as to relate (or not) to something else:

3. *Material and Semiotic Flows.* Here is the domain not only of speech but also of action, in a world understood less as one of things and more as one of processes, that is, things that appear in streams: signs, bean counters, money, libido, gasoline, semen, milk, electricity... The space of flows is taken by social science as the very realm of reality; institutions, economics, relations of classes, things we can measure – or even things that we can change. So this is the dreaded realm of acting out, where you move from intuition and upwelling desire to concrete statements and irrevocable deeds. These Flows of the Actually Real are as different from Virtual Territories as the word on the tip of your tongue is from the one you've just spoken. Yet the force of actuality relates them (or not) to something else:

4. *Abstract Machinic Phlya.* Now we arrive at the realm of the symbolic, of code, of formalised concepts: rhizomes of abstract ideas whose destiny is to complexify forever, like science, philosophy, mathematics, law, and everything that fills the Borgesian Library of Babel. The notion of the 'phylum', with its connotations of metamorphosis over time, is a way to indicate this evolutionary movement. As formalised codes, the machinic Phyla exist beneath the regime of the Actually Possible. They interact with the realm of material and semiotic Flows, not only through the dialectic of theory and practice, but also in a more estranging or deterritorialising relation where practice is pulled outside itself and into the endless labyrinth of ideas. Guattari seemed to think that abstract ideas have a direct relation (maybe not) to the glimmering of aesthetic universes.

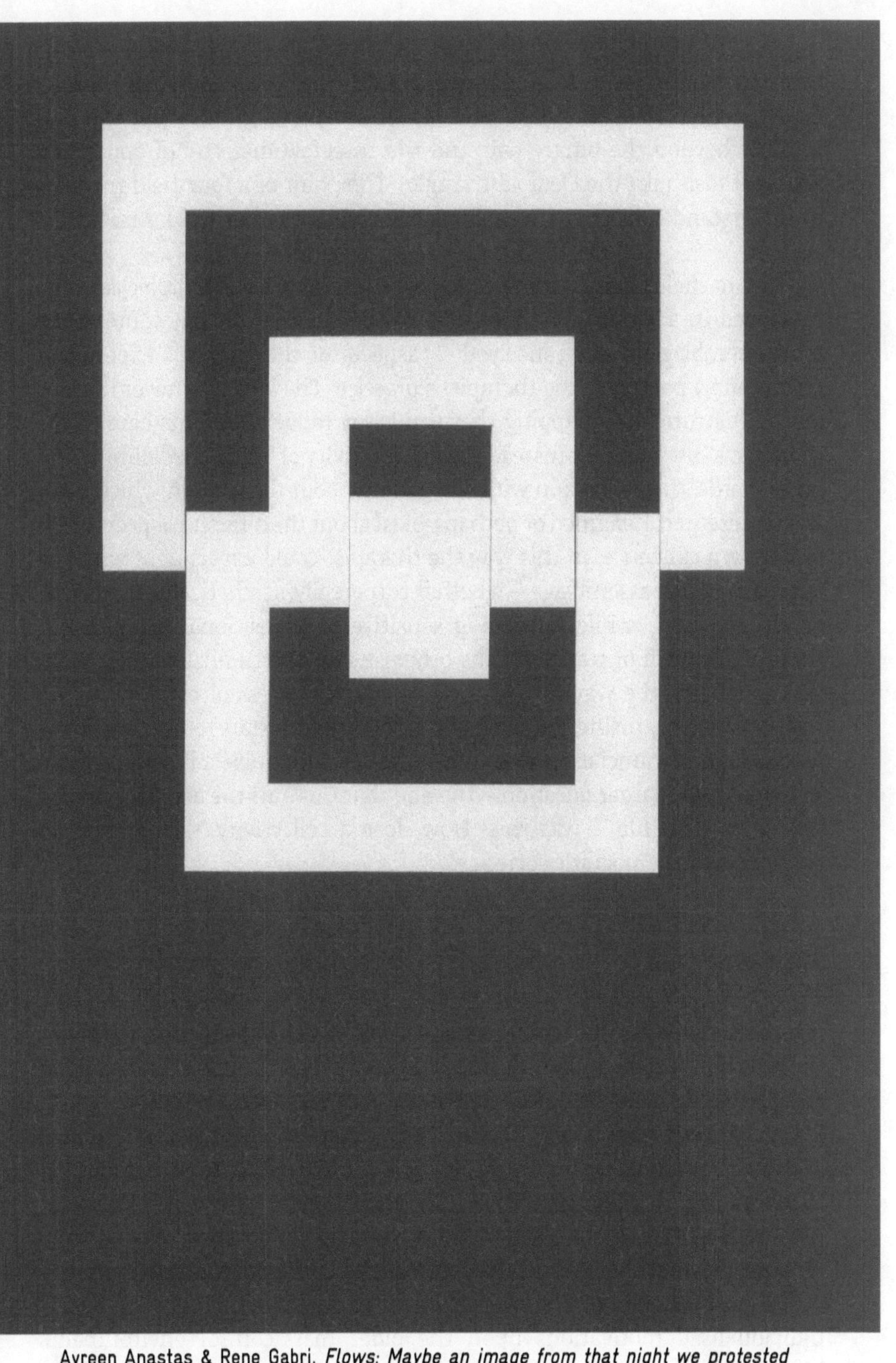

Ayreen Anastas & Rene Gabri, *Flows: Maybe an image from that night we protested in MoMA during WELCOME TO THE NEW PARADIGM or THE CRISIS OF EVERYTHING EVERYWHERE meetings, 2013*

Schizoanalysis offers four pathways into the complexity of human experience. It could also have been six or seventeen: four is just the first number beyond the binary pair and the threefold dialectic of opposition and synthesis (aka the Oedipal triangle). The point of a four-field model is to understand subjectivity as a generative matrix rather than a calculable system.

Before their formalisation as a book, the *Schizoanalytic Cartographies* were developed in a seminar with a group of therapists.[11] In that context, the four assemblages were conceived as aspects of the patient's experience, and as entry points for the therapist's practice. The idea was never to carry out an instrumental mapping that would lay hidden contents bare to the therapist's intervention. Instead it was an activity of 'meta-modelling', or in other words, a conversation with the patient about the ways in which he or she represented, imagined or perhaps joked about the different aspects of his or her own existence. In this way the therapist could experiment with the approach to one assemblage – whether corporeally, aesthetically, materially or discursively – while remaining sensitive to 'transitional components' that might touch or transform the others. As in structuralist activity, what was sought on the way in was the way out: an excess or overflow into a relation. By recognising the schiz of the self, you can start to hear a *collective* assemblage of enunciation, even when the speaking subject is ostensibly an individual. The larger question – the one that Guattari the activist pursued throughout his life – was this: How does a collectivity 'take speech' in contemporary democratic societies?

Your Way Out

It has become difficult to create what used to be called 'public space', that is, the possibility to articulate differing perspectives on a common condition. On the one hand, the structuralisation of the political process is now complete. Every national population is ceaselessly analysed, modelled, stimulated and then measured again for results by a narrow spectrum of competing/ collaborating interest groups, whose mouthpieces are called 'leaders'. Meanwhile, thanks essentially to finance and its proliferation of networked technologies, another wrinkle has been added to the programmed societies of the postwar period. The overlay of a vast and dynamic grid of hyper-individualised motivations upon the older mass-control environments has given rise to a new normalised figure, the *entrepreneur of the self*, whose boundlessly calculating opportunism and compulsive service-with-a-smile makes the 'fascist in your head' look seriously outdated. Today, the biggest obstacle to grassroots democracy is the well known impossibility of scheduling a face-to-face meeting to fit the calendars of five or more people. And so it becomes clear why there is such an intensive focus on the crisis-management of urban disasters, financial collapses, crimes, terrorism, wars, etc. The goal is to keep our clocks desynchronised, and to block the spontaneous collective response that a real emergency – like climate change or a *coup d'état* by the bankers – would otherwise provoke. Just-in-time production, with its intricate systems for sequencing the efforts of millions of workers who will never meet or even know what each other are doing, is only the living allegory of a broader neoliberal predicament.[12]

Let's redefine 'tactical media' as the art of breaking the strictly functional relays between the human microchips of the integrated social processor. Schizoanalysis would suggest that this is not going to be done by a totalising ideology, or even the wonderful old Wobblie dream of 'one big union'. Instead, actual assemblages are taken on their own terms, and dissociation is pushed to an excess. In the early days of OWS, protesters lay belly on the ground writing slogans and demands on cardboard. The by-passing businessmen thought they were completely nuts. Maybe they themselves thought they were completely nuts. Behind the incomprehension was a deliberate organisational process that aimed at the creation of a public general assembly. It did so by actually holding such assemblies, step by step over a couple of months leading up to the initial events on 17 September, 2011. The schiz on Wall Street became a catalyst for the taking of speech on national and global scales.

Notice that a schizoanalytic mapping would look for at least two different assemblages on the scene of these public protests. One is the existential territory of the street. In societies of controlled and captivated flows, the occupation of the street is an ecstatic discovery (maybe that's the reason for all the drumming). Along with the exceptional circumstance of thousands of people with nothing to focus on but each other, there is an invitation to a new mobility. A crowd moves with a multitude of legs and arms and eyes and tongues. It dances upon itself like a swarm of bees (the general assembly). Then it surges like an uncurling wave, whose powerful current (the protest march) can instantly scatter into glittering, self-reflexive spray (the flashing cameras). Subjectively, the territory of the street is a release from imposed privacy, a space of possibility, an opening of social desire. But on the objective level it is all about deliberation, organisation, communication, action. Some bodies made the meals, put together the library, facilitated the assembly, took the notes, did the dishes, set up the websites, wrote the communiqués, scouted out the scene and bore detailed witness to the police abuse. There is a rough-and-tumble technical precision to grassroots political events, not only in the electronic communications but in all the skill sets that are delivered over to collective elaboration. The key is deprofessionalisation, or the shift away from protected, quasi-sacralised circuits of exchange to a profane world of everyday use.[13] The occupation of the street – the opening of the existential territory – is what makes this difference.

Another difference is made where pragmatic activists would expect it the least: in the realm of social theory. Political action in a complex society is impossible without theory. First, the structures of everyday capitalist life and the strategies of those who impose them must be analysed, deciphered and correlated with the latest trends in technoscience, economics, governance and military practice. Next, the conclusions must be crafted into concepts that can be seized and used by those who do not make such things their speciality. This is not particularly easy. Theorising in, for and against the street is a tightrope act where the inevitable fall is not only openly desired by the crowd, but needed by the theorist as a reality check. Universities, where the acuity of thought is pursued most intensively, are not by accident a disciplinary space that seems dedicated to the ultimate neutralisation of all ideas. The communications machine of the social movement offers a test for those whose philosophy of praxis forbids an infinite delay of commitment in the search for theoretical perfection. If that machine can be thrown off the rails – if inquiry can remain open and sharp at the very heart of political urgency – then it is possible to go on mobilising for the next decisive phase of the endless revolution.

But we would miss something if we stuck only with the actual, the factual, the ultra-theoretical and the 'territories of the virtually real'. As Gary Genosko asks, 'What inspires a sixteen-year-old with a dead-end McJob to try to organize her fellow employees into a bargaining unit in the face of the intimidating power of a multinational known for union busting?'[14] No one knows the answer, and aesthetics is far too narrow a term for the siren songs of political desire. While emerging one morning from the subway in Brussels, on the day of a big demo, I realised that everyone around me was donning a mask, hoisting a sign, brandishing a puppet or readying some more complicated expressive machine – all no doubt in echo of subjective possibilities glimpsed elsewhere, in painting, in cinema, in literature or out in the street. It's clear that many artists, by plunging ever deeper into whatever

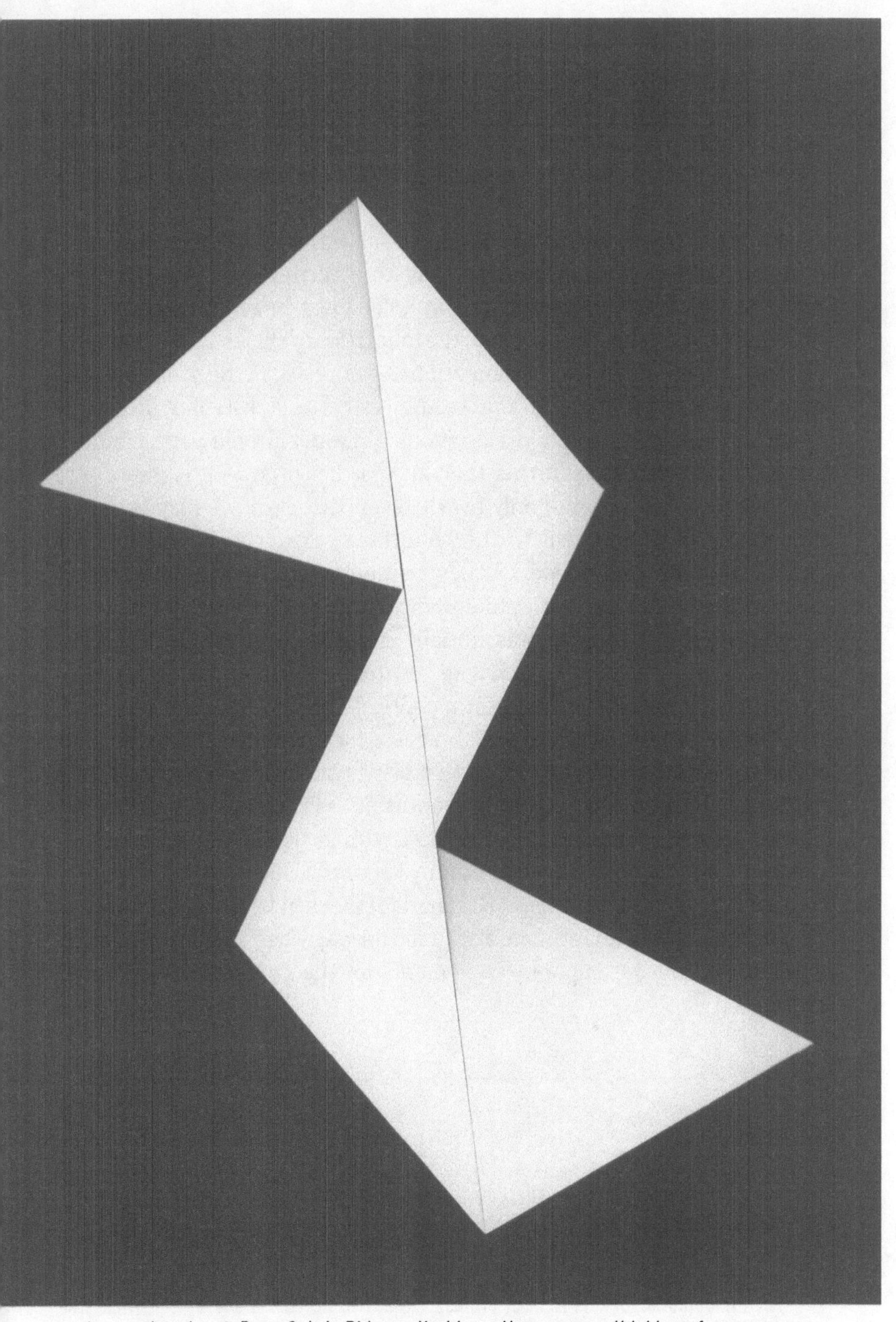

Ayreen Anastas & Rene Gabri, *Rhizomatic Ideas: Here we are thinking of one page from Rene's lost notebook from the Enigma of Capital*, 2013

they are striving to create, end up more politically aware than the most dedicated cadres, because they have kept a living link between perception and expression. If a latter day 'workers' self-inquiry' were ever able to reveal the sources of the precariat's dreams, we could expect immediate victory. Or mediated cooptation!

Events are moments when the map of subjectivity is at stake and can be transformed. This can happen all the way from micro-levels of the self to the world-historical events of wars, economic collapses, imperial conquests and revolutions. It can happen in any of the four fields of subjectivity, singularly, or more often, in complex combinations. Eventwork is the schizoanalysis of political activism. It doesn't proceed by fiat, but by listening. It doesn't marshal forces, but accepts dissociation. It doesn't simplify and channel, but overflows and filters further than any particular issue. It is the culture of the left and the key, not only to whatever 'successes' we may have and desperately need, but also to the continuing existence of the we that desires such things. This work is now being carried out with increasingly sophisticated organisational, philosophical and aesthetic resources, going beyond the limits of what was initially called 'tactical media.'[15] If what happened in 2011 is any indication, its territories will dramatically multiply in the upcoming decade of long-term political-economic crisis.

The present is no time to make excuses for sloppiness and failure. But at the same time, the social process that brings radically different aspects of existence together into a powerful event is not something one can entirely master. Like the Freudian dreamwork, it 'thinks' when you are not fully conscious, it 'acts' when you are not fully in control. Such is the challenge of multiplicity, or rule by the *demos*. Hundreds of thousands, perhaps millions of people know this in an intimate and practical way. Their grace and audacity is the breath of contemporary movements for the articulation of political speech.

Footnotes

1   For the initial formulation of this concept, see my text, 'Eventwork: The Fourfold Matrix of Contemporary Social Movements', in: Nato Thompson, (ed.), *Living as Form: Socially Engaged Art from 1991–2011* (MIT Press, 2012), http://brianholmes. wordpress.com/2012/02/17/eventwork.

2   For the definition of this form of protest art, see David Garcia and Geert Lovink, 'The ABC of Tactical Media', http://tinyurl.com/abc-of-tactical-media.

3   Félix Guattari, *Schizoanalytic Cartographies*, Andrew Goffey (trans.), London: Bloomsbury, 2013. The ideas subsequently attributed to Guattari all contain an inevitable dose of interpretation.

4   Cf. R. K. Merton and P. L. Kendall, 'The Focused Interview', *American Journal of Sociology* 51-6 (1946); Jay W. Forrester, *Industrial Dynamics*, Cambridge, MA: MIT Press, 1961; *World Dynamics* ,Cambridge, MA: Wright-Allen Press, 1971. On feedback techniques in the social sciences, see Karl Deutsch, *The Nerves of Government: Models of Political Communication and Control*, New York: Free Press, 1963; the author presents his own book in a short synopsis, available at http://tinyurl.com/nerves-of-government. For a critical look at cybernetic systems in the postwar period, see the final section of my book, *Escape the Overcode: Activist Art in the Control Society*, Zagreb and Eindhoven: WHW and Vanabbe Museum, 2009, at http://brianholmes.wordpress.com/2009/01/19/book-materials. And if you're not impressed by theory, see this newspaper article: www.nytimes.com/2013/02/24/magazine/the-extraordinary-science-of-junk-food.html.

5   Bruno Bosteels, 'What is an event?' Lecture delivered on 2 July 2012, at Documenta 13, Kassel, Germany. Video available for one year only: http://d13.documenta.de/#/research/research/view/lecture-what-is-thinking-or-a-taste-that-hates-itself-bruno-bosteels-what-is-an-event.

6   Étienne Balibar, 'Structuralism: A Destitution of the Subject?' in: *differences: A Journal of Feminist Cultural Studies* 14 :1 (2005), p.3.

7   Alain Touraine, *The Post-Industrial Society*, New York: Random House, 1971, p.5.

8   The concept of 'tactics' used by the Amsterdam theorists of tactical media is taken from one of the writers most closely associated with May '68, Michel de Certeau, *The Practice of Everyday Life*, Berkeley: UC Press, 1984/1st French ed. 1974.

9   Félix Guattari, Schizoanalytic Cartographies, op. cit., p.42.

10 Michel de Certeau, *La prise de parole: pour une nouvelle culture*, Paris: Desclée de Brouwer, 1968, translated as *The Capture of Speech*, University of Minnesota Press, 1998.

11 See '*Les séminaires de F.* Guattari 1980 – 1981', http://www.revue-chimeres.fr/drupal_chimeres/?q=node/143.

12 For more on just-in-time production, see my text 'Do Containers Dream of Electric People?' in: *Open* 21 2011, http://www.skor.nl/_files/Files/OPEN21EN_P30-44.pdf.

13 For a more detailed reading of deprofessionalisation, see my text, 'Profanity and the Financial Markets: A User's Guide to Closing the Casino', Documenta 13/Hatje Cantz Verlag, 2012, text available at http://brianholmes.wordpress.com/2012/01/02/profanity-and-the-financial-markets.

14 Gary Genosko, *Félix Guattari: An Aberrant Introduction*, London: Continuum, 2002, p.3.

15 For a polemical reflection on those limits, see my text 'Swarmachine: Activist Media Tomorrow', in *Escape the Overcode*, op. cit., http://brianholmes.wordpress.com/2007/07/21/swarmachine.

REMAKING MEDIA PRACTICES: FROM TACTICAL MEDIA TO POST-MEDIA

CLEMENS APPRICH

The assumption that 'old' media are not simply replaced but rather dialectically preserved by 'new' media is as old as media studies Itself. However, it is not only the sublation of the old into the new that characterises the development of media technologies, but the engagement with old media formats also leads on to a progression of practices that finally provide a new approach to these technologies. Thus, since the beginning of the 20th century, electronic media (radio, television, computer-based networks, etc.) have been affected by a constant interrelation between avant-garde experimentation and mass distribution. The following article will trace back some of the practices that have made use of new media technologies in order to bring about Guattari's idea of a post-media age: a transformation of classical media structures towards new collective assemblages of enunciation. In media theory, this process was accompanied by a dialectical movement: first in the 1980s, postmodern media theory jettisoned Marx's critique of ideology and abandoned all hope of an emancipatory use of media technologies, and then the tactical media movement of the 1990s rejected this quietist standpoint of (academic) media theory in order to re-invent new forms of media activism. This 'double disengagement' ultimately opened up new fields of counter-hegemonic agency, thus enabling a variety of media practices that are still valid in a post-media era. This article, therefore, follows the assumption that the transition from tactical media to post-media should not be considered as a rupture, but rather as a 'Becoming-media' of those practices that emerged in 1990s.[1] In this sense, the practices of tactical media have not disappeared but rather merged into everyday (post-media) life.

Baudrillard vs. Enzensberger – First Disengagement

According to French media theorist Jean Baudrillard the mass is 'no more than the zero degree of the political'[2] By this, Baudrillard means the 'zero degree' of social meaning, the dissolution of the political. Contrary to Marx's conception of a political mass movement, it is therefore irrelevant if the masses overcome their supposed alienation, because the mass itself is the place of this alienation. For Baudrillard, the mass has reached its culmination. It is accelerating towards its limit, which today is expressed as social implosion rather than a revolutionary explosion. This also applies in relation to mass media which, from a Marxist point of view, has long been considered a manipulative force:

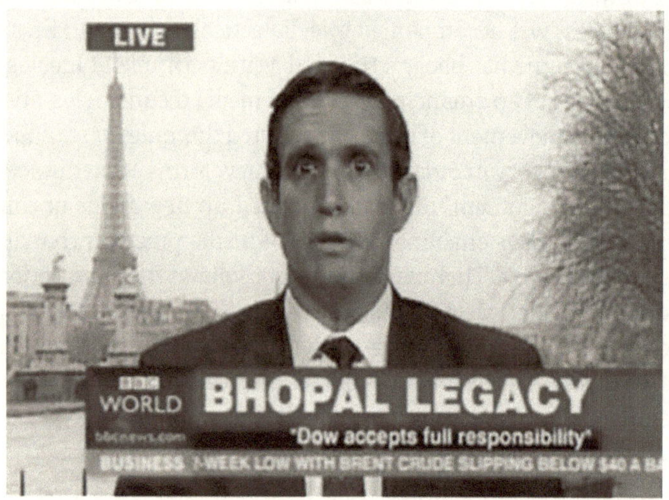

Television still of the Yes Men's Andy Bichlbaum on the BBC News, 2004

It has always been thought – this is the very ideology of the mass media – that it is the media which envelop the masses. The secret of manipulation has been sought in a frantic semiology of the mass media. But it has been overlooked, in this naive logic of communication, that *the masses are a stronger medium than all the media* [...].[3]

Hence, the masses must not be freed from the media, in order to unleash their revolutionary potential, but on the contrary, the media has to be freed from the masses. In this quietist view, the masses no longer produce the social, but rather simulate it. In the 'society of simulation' the social loses its meaning, thus rendering any political change impossible. This disengagement from the political programme of Marxism is not only in contradiction to the widespread suspicion within leftist theory which sees in (mass) media nothing more than (mass) manipulation, but also contrary to any hope for a socialist strategy of (re)appropriating (mass) media, as suggested by Hans Magnus Enzensberger's 'Contituents of a Theory of the Media.'[4]

In his essay, written in 1970, Enzensberger criticises the renunciation of an emancipatory use of new media technologies by members of the '68 generation. For him, it is clear that a socialist media theory has to appropriate the 'manipulative power' of the media if it does not want to be powerless against technological developments:

> [E]very use of the media presupposes manipulation. The most elementary processes in media production, from the choice of the medium itself to shooting, cutting, synchronization, dubbing, right up to distribution, are all operations carried out on the raw material. There is no such thing as unmanipulated writing, filming, or broadcasting. The question is therefore not whether the media are manipulated, but who manipulates them. A revolutionary plan should not require the manipulators to disappear; on the contrary, it must make everyone a manipulator.[5]

The electronic media, for Enzensberger, constitute a new productive force whose practical means are already in the hands of the masses. However, the dominant relations of production would suppress the 'mobilising power' of the media, thus leading to a de-politicisation of the masses: 'In its present form, equipment like television or film does not serve communication but prevents it. It allows no reciprocal action between transmitter and receiver'[6]. In this sense, the transition from a simple apparatus of distribution to a veritable tool of communication is not a technical but a political problem. In reference to Bertolt Brecht's 'Radio Theory', Enzensberger shows that every transistor radio is, by the nature of its construction, not only a receiver, but also a potential transmitter.[7] The maintained separation into transmitters and receivers therefore only mirrors 'the basic contradiction between the ruling class and the ruled class', between the consciousness industry and the controlled masses.[8]

According to Enzensberger, the division into producers and consumers is not inscribed into electronic media, but can be ascribed to the political, social and economic conditions of the capitalist system. In his argumentation, the Marxist phase model is clearly recognisable, according to which the continuously evolving forces of production (i.e. natural, technical, scientific, organisational and intellectual resources) are being trapped by the prevailing relations of production (i.e. relations of property, labour, distribution, circulation and consumption) and thus form a specific mode of production (e.g. bourgeois capitalism). So for Enzensberger it is obvious that electronic media are part of the economic-political structure, i.e. part of the material basis and not simply an outgrowth of the ideological superstructure:[9] 'With the development of the electronic media, the industry that shapes consciousness has become the pacemaker for the social and economic development of societies in the late industrial age'.[10] In order to free the emancipatory potential of the new productive forces from the dominant relations of production, a collective mode of production would be required that is oriented to the needs and interests of the masses. Given an often repeated, but usually insufficient critique of the emancipation hypotheses, it has to be said that Enzensberger is not simply talking about 'individual bricolage' (for instance in the basement hobby room of radio amateurs), but is underlining the importance of new organisational models:

> Networklike communications models built on the principle of reversibility of circuits might give indications of how to overcome this situation: a mass newspaper, written and distributed by its readers, a video network of politically active groups.[11]

Key to his argumentation is not the mere proliferation of media technologies, but their activation through an autonomous use of media tools.

In his response, Jean Baudrillard shares Enzensberger's opinion that it is not enough to simply turn every receiver into a transmitter in order to break the power of ruling media structures. However, for Baudrillard the mere reversal of the communication process is also insufficient, because 'reversibility has nothing to do with reciprocity.'[12] According to Baudrillard, the media structure itself prevents – regardless of the prevailing mode of production – any form of communication, because the apparatus transcends any 'real exchange' to the abstract level of the code. Transmitter and receiver can indeed change their position, but they thereby only reproduce the old pattern of communication, within which one can choose the code of the message and the other only has the choice to accept it or not. Hence, (electronic) media can not be (re-)appropriated for an emancipatory use. Instead Enzensberger calls for a replacement of the concept of (mass) media by one of radical immediacy:

> The street is, in this sense, the alternative and subversive form of the mass media, since it isn't, like the latter, an objectified support for answerless messages, a transmission system at a distance. It is the frayed space of the symbolic exchange of speech – ephemeral, mortal: a speech that is not reflected on the Platonic screen of the media.[13]

Hence, a true 'revolution of signs' can ultimately only occur outside of mass media, as Baudrillard attempts to show by the example of graffiti.[14] Only the direct 'insurrection and eruption in the urban landscape as the site of the reproduction of the code' allows a collective production that is able to prevent a separation between producers and consumers, between transmitters and receivers.[15]

According to Baudrillard, it is therefore no coincidence that the 'media revolution' has not taken place yet, because the possibility of such a revolution 'presupposes an upheaval in the entire existing structure of the media.'[16] Accordingly, only singular 'symbolic actions' are possible, which may irritate the ruling system, but cannot overcome it. It is because of this quietism that Oliver Marchart sees in Baudrillard's approach yet another version of the manipulation thesis, namely at the point 'where criticism of ideology turns into subversive affirmation.'[17] This raises the question of political agency, which is not captured by a determinist definition of the media. Both the deep suspicion towards the manipulative power of the media (manipulation paradigm), as well as the wide-eyed hope of its emancipatory potential (emancipation paradigm) ultimately cleave to the idea that social change (positive or negative) can be directly derived from technological structures: 'In both cases, however with reversed signs, the argumentation tends to "technicist' reductions."[18] A way out of this quandary, according to Marchart, arises from a third paradigm of Marxist media theory: namely that of politics, which considers media as hegemonic apparatuses.

Tactical Media – Second Disengagement

A non-deterministic theory of media tries to free itself from a manipulation paradigm beyond remedy, as well as from a too optimistic emancipation paradigm by emphasising the paradigm of politics. In this sense, it is no longer a question of whether the media by the nature of their construction are manipulative or emancipatory, but to what extent media can be understood as hegemonic apparatuses. Thus the media take on greater significance in this perspective: 'As hegemonic apparatuses of civil society they are both, terrain as well as means of self-assertion within a hegemonic struggle of position.'[19] What function they finally fulfil is never determined a priori, but arises from the 'trench warfare' over cultural hegemony. All the more, as media are transporting social knowledge (in terms of images, values, categories, classifications and lifestyles) and therefore contribute to the construction of hegemonic identity.[20] The concept of hegemony, coined by Antonio Gramsci, refers to a politically produced consensus that constitutes the common sense of a given historical period. Hegemony serves as a link between civil society (which rules through consent) and political society (which rules through force), leading to the well known formula: 'State = political society + civil society, in other words hegemony protected by the armour of coercion.'[21] Control over the state's coercive apparatus (especially the police, the judiciary and the military) does not of itself guarantee the preservation of political power – rather, it requires the 'voluntary consent' of the subordinate population in order to consolidate power.

Hegemony therefore describes the ability of dominant groups or classes to establish their own interests so that they are ultimately considered as the general interest by subaltern groups and classes. Such a 'consent of the governed' implies either the explicit approval of existing social relations, ideas and practices or at least their passive acceptance. Nonetheless, this is not necessarily a harmonic balance of interests, but rather a 'condensation' of social struggles.[22] The resolution of these struggles takes place via social compromise, within which the relevant (i.e. articulated) interests are constantly renegotiated. Hence, the access to media technologies in order to articulate those interests takes on greater significance. Civil society becomes the preferred terrain on which hegemony arises, but it is also the place where counter-hegemonic concepts can evolve. It is in this regard that one can look on media as political instruments: 'The emancipatory (or the manipulative) therefore can be found in emancipatory (or manipulative) politics, not in the apparatus.'[23] This implies a shift in the question: what is of interest

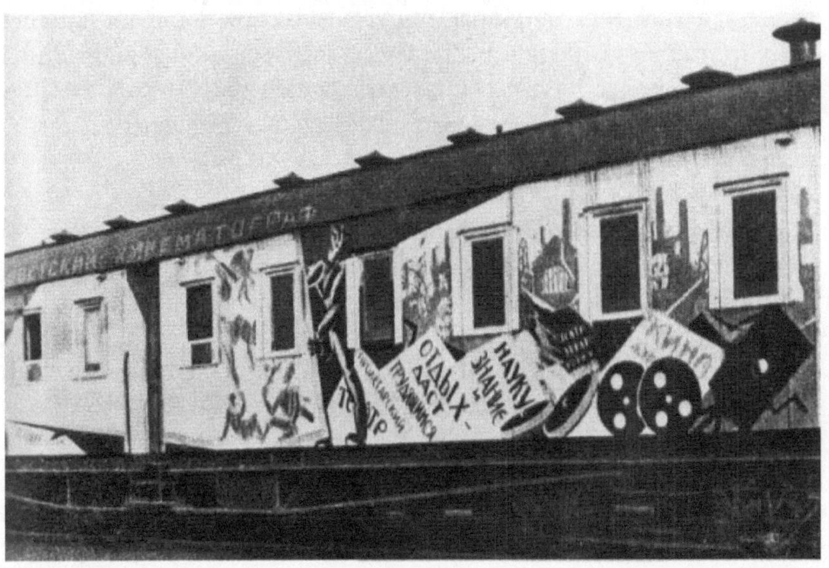

Agitational propaganda train used to spread revolutionary ideas to far flung Russian countryside

is not the (optimistic or pessimistic) deduction of social practices from the technological structure, but rather the power relations within society.

An essential part of hegemonic power entails the ability to present the status quo as being without alternatives – whether people are content with it or simply give up hope, does not make a difference for the exercise of power.[24] The ruling hegemony materialises in state institutions and becomes the basis for legislative and executive decisions. Accordingly, the potential of emancipatory agency to challenge the discursive framework is as important as the ability to act on the institutional terrain itself. By implication, counter-hegemonic actions also cannot be represented by civil society as a whole because it is not located outside of the dominant state, but rather contributes (through media, associations, educational and cultural institutions, etc.) to its constitution and reproduction. Thus, alternative notions and ideas initially emerge in small sectors of civil society, not in its most powerful ones:

> What matters is the criticism to which such an ideological complex is subjected by the first representatives of the new historical phase. This criticism makes possible a process of differentiation and change in the relative weight that the elements of the old ideologies used to possess. What was previously secondary and subordinate, or even incidental, is now taken to be primary – becomes the nucleus of a new ideological and theoretical complex. The old collective will dissolves into its contradictory elements since the subordinate ones develop socially, etc.'[25]

The state and the general public remain significant areas of political struggle, but they are not necessarily at the centre of it. Counter-hegemonic agency is rather about a self-positioning in the wide field of hegemony.

Such an assertive self-positioning also was central to 'tactical media' – a new form of media criticism which, after the fall of the Berlin Wall, spread across Europe (and beyond). One of the 'birthplaces' of tactical media was the Amsterdam festival Next Five Minutes (N5M) where, in the early and mid-1990s, a new generation of internet activists encountered an older generation of radio and video activists leading to a shift of definition concerning media activism.[26] 'The ABC of Tactical Media', a quasi-manifesto written by David Garcia and Geert Lovink, states:

> Tactical Media are what happens when the cheap >do it yourself< media, made possible by the revolution in consumer electronics and expanded forms of distribution (from public access cable to the internet) are exploited by groups and

individuals who feel aggrieved by or excluded from the wider culture. Tactical media do not just report events, as they are never impartial they always participate and it is this that more than anything separates them from mainstream media.[27]

This already points to the fact that in the struggle for hegemonic power a leading role was assigned to new media technologies in the 1990s. However, the idea of 'do it yourself' media is as old as 'community media' which emerged in the 1960s in order to represent social, cultural and ethnic minority interests. Particularly in the US, new legal requirements that obliged commercial cable TV-stations to reserve at least one channel for non-commercial programmes provided a technological and financial basis for independent broadcasting. And during the 1970s video technology developed apace, resulting in the so-called 'camcorder revolution' of the 1980s.[28]

In Europe, especially those places where a lively scene of 'pirate TV and radio stations' already existed (e.g. Amsterdam, Berlin, London, Bologna, Vienna but also Ljubljana and Riga), independent internet providers (such as the Digital City Amsterdam or the International City of Berlin) emerged with the introduction of the WWW in the mid-1990s. Because of these initiatives, as well as a further fall in the price of information and communication technologies (primarily the PC, but also cheaper net access), the internet was finally implemented as a mass medium. At that point, a new generation of media activists was born: 'They radicalised the ideas of community media by challenging everyone to produce their own media in support of their own political struggles.'[29] In this sense, one could speak of a second disengagement: while postmodern media theory of the 1980s (Baudrillard, Kittler, Bolz, etc.) turned away from a Marxist critique of ideology, the 1990s witnessed a rejection of this 'speculative media theory' in order to invent new emancipatory forms of counter-hegemonic agency.[30] This 'double disengagement' from a classical media theory which posits media as the tool of ideological programming therefore opened up a new theoretical perspective to the effect that it was no longer only about the reflection on media conditions, but rather about the co-creation of these conditions ('Media determine our situation' as Friedrich Kittler famously said). This is why Geert Lovink, one of the initiators of the N5M, writes in retrospect:

Jean Baudrillard's elaborations on simulation were useful in the 1980s when the media scape exploded. Approaching the millennium everything seemed simulated and Baudrillard's elaborations started to sound conservative and out of touch with the actual Internet reality.[31]

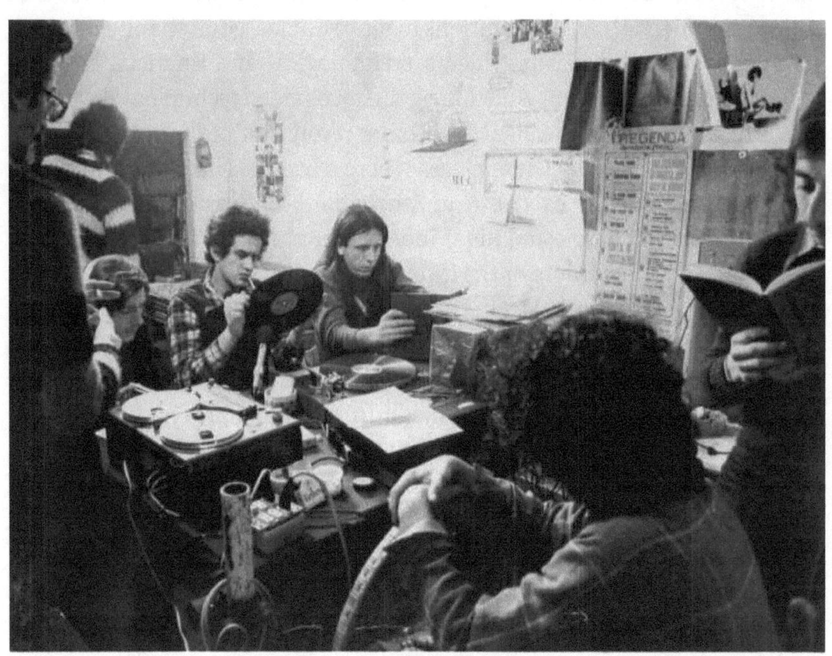

Radio Alice, free radio station broadcasting from Bologna in the late 1970s and closed by the carabinieri, 12 March 1977

In order to distinguish themselves from the academic critique of (mass) media, tactical media theorists considered their practices as 'digital micro-politics.'[32]

Post-Media Strategies

Tactical media describe an ensemble of practices that are located at the intersection of art, theory, politics, culture, activism, technology and media. This pluralistic approach not only challenges the idea of specialisation but was indeed seen as a liberating process by tactical media activists in the 1990s: 'There was a feeling of relief that those involved in tactical media could be any kind of cultural hybrid. [...] Many felt liberated from having to present themselves to the public as a specialist in order to be experts.'[33] And as the Critical Art Ensemble (CAE) note in their book on tactical media, it is precisely this 'aversion to boredom caused by redundant specialized activity' that urges people to challenge the existing order by creative means.[34] In this sense, tactical media are not limited solely to digital technology, but include all forms of old and new media in order to achieve counter-hegemonic goals. What is important in this context, is the collective appropriation of different media formats, in order to produce new forms of knowledge: '[R]ather than just doing critical reading and theorizing, [tactical media] practitioners go on to develop participatory events that demonstrate the critique through an experiential process.'[35] Tactical media therefore positions itself outside the traditional institutions (i.e. universities, academic research institutions, municipal museums, galleries, political foundations, cultural and media centres), not least because the generated knowledge should be used to challenge hierarchical structures and to open up new realms of possibilities beyond these institutions.[36]

The idea of a collective and non-institutionalised appropriation of media culture as well as the joint experimentation with new information and communication technologies has given rise to a (global) movement challenging dominant (media) structures:

> For a brief time there was and continues to be a relief from capital's tyranny of specialization that forces us to perform as if we are a fixed set of relationships and characteristics, and to repress or strictly manage all other forms of desire and expression.[37]

In this context, CAE's concept of a 'liberating collective arrangement of enunciation' refers to the work of Félix Guattari who, in the 1980s, already nourished the hope that collective forms of articulation could replace the old passifying media structures. In accordance with a non-deterministic conception of media, he underlines the fact that the spur of change resides in social practices, not in the technological structure itself: 'Obviously, we cannot expect a miracle from these technologies: it will all depend, ultimately, on the capacity of groups of people to take hold of them, and apply them to appropriate ends.'[38] Linked to this statement is the question of whether and how self-organised networks can preserve their autonomy against mass media.[39] Acting contrarily to mass media, which tends to reproduce a consensual (i.e. normative) subjectivity, alternative media – according to Guattari – enable the creation of new modes of subjectivation: 'We are currently witnessing a mutuation of subjectivity that perhaps surpasses the invention of writing, or the printing press, in importance.'[40] However, this new form of a 'computer-aided subjectivity' is not the simple result of technological change, but rather a manifestation of micro-politics that emerged in the wake of new media appropriation.[41]

Guattari considers the formation of these micro-politics as an immanent process of becoming, which itself should be experienced as a process of greater freedom. Similar to tactical media, Guattari's motivation is to escape the 'postmodern impasse.'[42] He is concerned with the possibility of an individual and collective (self-)positioning that can serve as a starting point for a new 'post-media era' in which 'the media will be reappropriated by a multitude of 'subject-groups.'[43] The proliferation of a media-based subjectivity therefore would not necessarily mean a further step towards the dissolution of the social (cf. Baudrillard), but could enable a recombination of social practices. Such a (re-)articulation of the social, which is opposed to postmodern quietism, refers to the fundamental openness of any 'social order' – even if this order is created by hegemonic strategies, it can never be completely constituted because of the continuing differences within the social.[44] This is why tactical media practices continue to play a crucial role, particularly since the 'strategic illusion vis-à-vis the media'[45] is just – according to Guattari – the most tangible symptom of a deeper crises: 'The suggestive power of the theory of information has contributed to masking the importance of the enunciative dimensions of communication.'[46] Messages are not transmitted alone, rather their meaning depends on the interpretative framework of each recipient.

In addition to the physical structure of the media (i.e. its code), environmental, social and mental aspects now move to the centre of interest to master the current mass media crisis:[47] 'Across Guattari's three ecological registers, the environment, the social relation, and human subjectivity, technology plays an integral role in intensifying the crisis, but simultaneously the arena where new solutions must be found.'[48] In his essay on the 'legacies of tactical media' Eric Kluitenberg refers to the media ecological debate of the 1990s that came up through the engagement with Guattari's work. In this sense, the massive dissemination of digital networks and internet technologies opened up a new 'ecological' field, on which new forms of cooperation and exchange, production and distribution have emerged. Based on Deleuze and Guattari's concept of the 'war machine', a systematic description of the media ecology was attempted:

> The media ecology is a machine composed of several distinct levels: the levels of media and related tools and instruments; the level of tactics, in which individuals and media are integrated into formations; the level of strategy, in which the campaigns conducted by those formations acquire a unified political goal; and finally, the level of logistics, of procurement and supply networks, in which media practice is connected to the infrastructural and industrial resources that fuel it.[49]

And even though the tactical media of the 1990s were mainly characterised by their temporary nature, they did not act in a purely virtual space, but rather tried to implement opportunities, which were created by new media technologies, in real society. This meant, for instance, that the development of infrastructure (especially in the form of self-managed servers) was deemed important, in order to be able to support cultural, social and political initiatives.

This strategic direction distinguishes these early netpioneers from current (resistant) media practices. Today, digital media technologies have become more prevalent than ever before, and as a consequence, tactical media practices (like remixing, sharing and producing media content) have penetrated almost all aspects of everyday life: 'With the advent of commercial hosting companies for blogs or videos [...] it has become very simple to shoot, edit and distribute rich media to audiences large and small.'[50] However, most of the media infrastructure we are using is in the hands of a few companies, thus re-establishing the old model of mass media domination: 'At the same time, the commercial capture of the infrastructure is creating new bottlenecks where censorship and control of media can and does function efficiently.'[51] In other words, the decentralisation of the means of production was accompanied by a centralisation of the relations of production. Due to this paradox, the interest in building up autonomous resources, networks and infrastructure has become more topical than ever. The point here is not so much to grow an alternative to conventional (mass) media, but rather to create one's own media in order to rearticulate the hegemonic field. As Guattari telegraphed,

> Refusing the status of the current media, combined with a search for new social interactivities, for an institutional creativity and an enrichment of values, would already constitute an important step on the way to a remaking of social practices.[52]

In order to be able to do so, a post-media strategy is required that considers media neither as external structure in terms of the manipulation or emancipation paradigm, nor as mere means in the struggle for political objectives, but as tools to shape our own everyday lives.

Footnotes

1   Joseph Vogl, 'Becoming-Media. Galileo's Telescope', *Grey Room*, Fall 2007, no. 29, pp.14–25.

2   Jean Baudrillard, *In the Shadow of the Silent Majorities…or the End of the Social*, New York, Semiotext(e), 1983, p.18

3   Ibid. p.44

4   One of the most prominent examples in this respect is Max Horkheimer and Theodor Adorno's essay 'The Culture Industry: Enlightenment as Mass Deception' in *Dialectic of Enlightenment*, Stanford University Press, 2002, which was published in the beginning of the 1940s. In it the two founders of the Frankfurt School identify (mass) media as part of the more broadly defined culture industries. In their view, culture industries are responsible for the industrial standardisation of the cultural field, therefore hindering the formation of autonomous individuals. Culture is reduced to advertising, i.e. the unquestioned acceptance of the existing situation: 'It is not only the standardized mode of production of the culture industry which makes the individual illusory in its products. Individuals are tolerated only as far as their wholehearted identity with the universal is beyond question. [...] [O]nly because individuals are none but mere intersections of universal tendencies is it possible to reabsorb them smoothly into the universal' (Horkheimer/Adorno 2002, p.124.). The reception of Adorno and Horkheimer's work during the protests of 1968 had a great influence on the understanding of media technologies by leftist groups. In Germany particualrly, the discussion was for a long time influenced by the idea that technology is the sole cause of instrumental domination, a fact that

finally prevented any critcial examination of these technologies; Hans Magnus
Enzensberger, 'Constituents of a Theory of the Media', in *The New Media Reader*,
Noah Wardrip-Fruin and Nick Montfort (eds.), Cambridge/London, MIT Press, 2003,
p.261–275.

5   Ibid. p.265

6   Ibid. p.262.

7   Bertolt Brecht, *'The Radio as an Apparatus of Communication'*, 1932, in Media.Art.Net,
http://www.medienkunstnetz.de/source-text/8

8   Ibid. p.262; The term 'consciousness industry' is basically in accord with the 'culture
industry' (above).

9   The base-superstructure theorem is one of the essential concepts in Marxist
theory, according to which the economic structure of a society (i.e. the totality of
the relations of production which correspond to a certain development stage of
the productive forces) provides the basis for the political, legal and ideological
superstructure (i.e. the state and religious institutions, but also moral ideas).
Thus, in 'The German Ideology – Ideology in General', (1844–46), Marx and Engels
write about human consciousness: 'Morality, religion, metaphysics, and all the
rest of ideology and their corresponding forms of consciousness no longer seem
to be independent. They have no history or development. Rather, men who develop
their material production and their material relationships alter their thinking
and the products of their thinking along with their real existence. Consciousness
does not determine life, but life determines consciousness. In the first view the
starting point is consciousness taken as a living individual; in the second it is the
real living individuals themselves as they exist in real life, and consciousness is
considered only as their consciousness', in *Marx on Religion*, John Raines (ed.),
Temple University Press, 2002, p.100. However, the relationship between base and
superstructure, as Marx and Engels understood it, is not simply a causal relation,
but a dialectical one.

10 Op. cit. p261.

11 Ibid. p.267. As Noah Wardrip-Fruin notes in his brief introduction to Enzensberger's
text, this passage resembles the concept of the 'rhizome' (cf. *A Thousand Plateaus*,
Gilles Delezuze and Félix Guattari, University of Minnesota Press, 1987) with
which Gilles Deleuze and Félix Guattari present an alternative model of knowledge
production and representation of the world. The rhizome is based on the 'principles
of connection and heterogeneity: any point of a rhizome can be connected to anything
other, and must be', ibid., p. 51. In the wake of the 'counter-globalisation movement'
of the 1990s the rhizome then became a metaphor for the netlike information and
organisation structure of the protests that made use of new media technologies: 'In
this case, new media have been used both to support the alternative organization
of a social movement (more a network than a hierarchy) and to provide a different
model of media consumption', Wardrip-Fruin, in ibid., p.260.

12 Jean Baudrillard, 'Requiem for the Media', *The New Media Reader*, ibid., p.286.

13 Ibid. p.283.

14 Jean Baudrillard, 'KOOL KILLER ou l'insurrection par les signes', *Interférences* (No.
3), Fall 1975.

15 Ibid., p.80. In his essay 'Immediatism' Hakim Bey, whose concept of the 'Temporary
Autonomous Zone' had a great impact on the youth and protest culture of the 1990s,
claims something similar when he emphasises the importance of new forms of

playful immediacy: 'Immediatism is not a movement in the sense of an aesthetic program. It depends on situation, not style or content, message or School. It may take the form of any kind of creative play which can be performed by two or more people, by and for themselves, face-to-face and together. In this sense it is like a game, and therefore certain rules may apply', Hakim Bey, T.A.Z. *The Temporary Autonomous Zone, Ontological Anarchy, Poetic Terrorism*, Autonomedia, 1991, p.10. Which kind of 'rules' these are, however, is not more fully explained.

16   Baudrillard, 'Requiem for the Media', op. cit., p.281.

17   The author translated this and the following quotes by Oliver Marchart. Oliver Marchart, 'Marx und Medien – Eine Einführung' *Schröter*, Jens/Schwering, Gregor/Stäheli, Urs (ed.): *Media Marx. Ein Handbuch*, Bielefeld (transcript), 2006, pp.45-58.

18   Ibid. p.52.

19   Ibid., p.53.

20   Stuart Hall, '"The Rediscovery of 'Ideology": Return of the Repressed in Media Studies', in *Cultural Theory and Popular Culture – A Reader*, John Storey, (ed.), Essex: Pearson, p.124-155.

21   Antonio Gramsci, *Selections from the Prison Notebooks of Antonio Gramsci*, New York: International Publishers, 1992, p.263.

22   Cf. Nicos Poulantzas, *State, Power, Socialism*, London/New York: Verso, 2000.

23   Marchart, op. cit., p.55.

24   One may be reminded of Margaret Thatcher's famous statement 'There is no alternative' which underlined her belief that economic liberalism, free trade and a neoliberal globalisation are the best ways for modern societies to develop. In 1992 political scientist Francis Fukuyama published his book 'The End of History and the last Man' (Fukuyama 1992) in which he argued that free market capitalism – after the collapse of Real Socialism – is without any alternative.

25   Gramsci, op. cit., p.195.

26   The conference series Next Five Minutes (N5M), which focused on issues related to art, activism and new media technologies, took place four times in total: The first edition, held in January 1993, was still under the influence of the events that followed the collapse of Real Socialism in Central and East European countries. In March 1996, the second N5M dealt with the onset of the early internet boom. Just before the Kosovo conflict, in March 1999, the third N5M addressed the issues of modern media wars, as they had become apparent during the First Iraq War in 1991. The last edition of N5M, held in September 2003, examined the effects of 9/11 on social movements. Despite the far-reaching influence of N5M, the festival never had regularly scheduled meetings or an institutionalised structure. Cf. Geert Lovink, *Zero Comments: Blogging and Critical Internet Culture*, New York/London: Routledge, 2008, p.187.

27   David Garcia and Geert Lovink, 'The ABC of Tactical Media', nettime mailinglist, 1997,: http://www.nettime.org/Lists-Archives/nettime-l-9705/msg00096.html. The term 'tactical media' refers directly to the analytical distinction made by Michel de Certeau, 'I call a 'strategy' the calculus of force-relationships which becomes possible when a subject of will and power (a proprietor, an enterprise, a city, a scientific institution) can be isolated from an 'environment.' A strategy assumes a place that can be circumscribed as *proper (propre)* and thus serve as the basis for generating relations with an exterior distinct from it (competitors, adversaries, 'clienteles', 'targets', or 'objects' of research). Political, economic, and scientific

rationality has been constructed on this strategic model. I call a 'tactic', on the other hand, a calculus which cannot count on a 'proper' (a spatial or institutional localization), nor thus on a borderline distinguishing the other as a visible totality. The place of a tactic belongs to the other. A tactic insinuates itself into the other's place, fragmentarily, without taking it over in its entirety, without being able to keep it at distance. It has at its disposal no base where it can capitalize on its advantages, prepare its expansions, and secure independence with respect to circumstances.' See, *The Practice of Everyday Life*, Berkeley: Universtiy of California Press, 1988, p.xix.

28   Felix Stalder, '30 Years of Tactical Media', in *Public Netbase: Non Stop Future. New Practices in Art and Media*, kuda.org (ed.), Frankfurt a. M.: Revolver, 2008, p.190–194.

29   Ibid., p.192.

30   Geert Lovink, *Dark Fiber. Tracking Critical Internet Culture*, Cambridge/London: MIT Press, 2002, p.23.

31   Ibid., p.266.

32   Ibid., p.255. According to Foucault, the 'microphysics of power' is relational, a power circulating between bodies, entities and institutions that cannot be fixed in terms of a specific system of rules. Hence, also the state is ultimately a manifestation of these power practices and contingent forces. Not only coercion and violence constitute the respective balance of power, but equally freedom, self-determination and consensual forms of action. Similar to Gramsci, Foucault states: 'I don't claim at all that the State apparatus is unimportant, but it seems to me that [...] power isn't localised in the State apparatus and that nothing in society will be changed if the mechanisms of power that function outside, below and alongside the State apparatuses, on a much more minute and everyday level, are not also changed.' See, Michel Foucault, *Power/Knowledge. Selected Interview and Other Writings 1972–1977*, New York: Pantheon Books, 1980, p.60.

33   Critical Art Ensemble, *Digital Resistance: Explorations in Tactical Media*, Brooklyn: Autonomedia, 2001, p.5.

34   Ibid., p.6.

35   Ibid., p.8.

36   Lovink, *Dark Fibre*, op. cit., p.254.

37   Critical Art Ensemble, op. cit., p.6.

38   Félix Guattari, 'Remaking Social Practices', in *The Guattari Reader*, Gary Genosko (ed.), Oxford/Cambridge: Blackwell, p.262–272.

39   In particular, the autonomous radio stations of the 1970s and 1980s represent for Guattari an example of how 'collective assemblages of enunciation' can be produced and preserved. For instance, Radio Alice (1976-77), a collectively operated radio station in Bologna, adopted a two-fold strategy: on the one hand, the programme was created by as many groups and individuals as possible, on the other hand, these groups and individuals were not allowed to speak on the behalf of other groups or individuals – at the same time a universalisation of access and a singularisation of expression. Cf. Radio Alice, *Collective A/travers* (1977), Brooklyn: Pétroleuse Press.

40   Ibid., p.268.

41   Félix Guattari, 'The Three Ecologies', in *new formations* (No. 8), Summer 1989, p.133.

42   Félix Guattari, 'The Postmodern Impasse', in: Genosko, op. cit., pp.109–113.

43   Guattari, 'The Three Ecologies', op. cit., p.144.

44 Such a conception of the social considers social entities as generally open and indeterminate: None of them has absolute validity in the sense of establishing a social space or a structural moment which, in turn, could not again be undermined. Because 'in a closed system of relational identities, in which the meaning of each moment is absolutely fixed, there is no place whatsoever for a hegemonic practice.' See, Ernesto Laclau and Chantal Mouffe, *Hegemony and Socialist Strategy: Towards a Radical Democratic Politics*, London/New York: Verso, p.134. It is crucial in this context that any kind of hegemonic power is ultimately constructed in a pragmatic way – power therefore is never essential, but relational.

45 Baudrillard, *Requiem for the Media*, op. cit., p.284.

46 Guattari, 'Remaking Social Practices', op. cit., p.266.

47 Recently this crisis became visible in the European protests against the 'Anti-Counterfeiting Trade Agreement' (ACTA), a multinational treaty for the purpose of establishing international standards for intellectual property rights enforcement. For a big part of the so called 'internet-generation' this treaty was perceived as a direct attack on their way of life but also as a symptom of the corruptness of 'the' system as a whole. After decades of (more or less academic) debates about the status of intellectual property rights in the age of digital media, these protests finally brought tens of thousands of (mainly young) people onto the streets and marked a crucial point in the politicisation of this generation.

48 Eric Kluitenberg, 'Legacies of Tactical Media: The Tactics of Occupation: From Tompkins Square to Tahrir, Amsterdam' (Network Notebooks), 2011, p.21. http://networkcultures.org/_uploads/NN5_EricKluitenberg.pdf

49 Andreas Broeckmann, 'Tactical Media/Media Ecology', in N5M, 1995, http://www.n5m.org/n5m2/media/texts/abroeck.html

50 Felix Stalder, op. cit., p.193.

51 Ibid.

52 Guattari, 'Remaking Social Practices', op. cit., p.272.

EMERGING TECHNO-ECOLOGICAL ART PRACTICES: TOWARDS RENEWABLE FUTURES

RASA SMITE AND RAITIS SMITS

Introduction

This text explores the growing tendency in contemporary media art to address and work with sustainability issues from mixed perspectives – social, cultural, ecological and technological. We suggest that more than just a new trend, this is evidence of an ongoing and fundamental shift from a 'techno-scientific' to a 'techno-ecological' paradigm. It is more than a coincidence that artists who have a background in digital media are among those who today are in the vanguard of the quest for a sustainable future. On the one hand, we can claim that this emerging tendency is the progeny of so called 'new media art' practices that arrived along with the internet culture in the '90s. It has been influenced by both: not only developments in new media technologies but also the internet's affordance of process, feedback and collective creation. Yet on the other hand, as we would also like to discuss an ecological perspective here, we suggest that it is important to follow other lines of development in modern and postmodern art practices of the 20th century; to name just a few examples such as the Land Art movement, begun in the late 1960s, or Joseph Beuys's *7000 Oaks* (1982). Accordingly, in order to analyse and contextualise emerging 'techno-ecological' art practices, our text retraces several parallel lines of development in 20th century art practices, as well as studying those media theories which suggest paradigms other than techno-determinism, for instance, 'post-media'. In this context we will be providing case studies of renewable network artist practices, including our own work created together with RIXC, as well as techno-ecological projects by other artists, thereby concretising the outlines of the suggested techno-ecological paradigm.

To Grow or Not to Grow

'To grow or not to grow, that is the question' – was the message by an unknown author submitted on the internet for the live 'long-bean' plant that was growing in an exhibition space in Tallinn. In 2010 when we launched our plant communication network project *Talk to Me*, our intention was to establish a dialogue with the part of society who share the same interest in a sustainable future. By using artistic language that is based on 'post-human' / 'post-medial' means of expression (living plants, web-interface, computer-generated voice) our attempt was to raise their awareness about the complexity of relations between people, nature and technology.

Ecology today can't be reduced to environmental issues alone. Neither can modern technology still be seen as the evil and primary cause of environmental disasters. Instead, there is an urgent need to build a new perspective which we call 'techno-ecological' that takes all this complexity into account.[1] Therefore art, which in the past often maintained its autonomous position, is now also leaving it for the sake of the quest for sustainability. And it is not a coincidence that artists, who once were deeply engaged in exploring the frontiers of digital media, are among those who are looking for new ideas and approaches to building a more sustainable world. Beyond this, we claim that art may play an important role in the quest for sustainability. Especially art which is rooted in the new media culture – with its process-based approach, collective creation and ability to establish (social) feedback – contains the potential to play a catalytic role. These emerging techno-ecological art practices often act as connectors – they cross and bridge different fields, social groups, human and non-human worlds – whereas their artistic language is the key factor and the 'short cut' that helps to establish a dialogue with society, to reach its consciousness and to create feedback with it.

From New Media to Post-Media

For a long time throughout the 19th and 20th centuries two lines of technological development ran in parallel – modern media and computing – without ever crossing paths. They all begin around the same time, as Lev Manovich argues: 'mass media and data processing are complementary technologies; they appear together and develop side by side, making modern mass society possible.'[2] It was nearly the end of the 20th century when these two separate lines of development finally met each other and merged with a third one – telecommunication technologies, as a result of which a new type of media was born: the internet. Only since the advent of the internet can we talk about the conditions of 'new media' – which is not new because the technology is new, but which is new conceptually. Hence, when all lines of the development of modern technologies finally converged and new media – the internet – emerged, alongside it a new paradigm for the development of modern society was born. This we can witness today when all the other old media machines and communications systems are now being digitised, including the production process which has been computerised, and distribution which is globally networked.

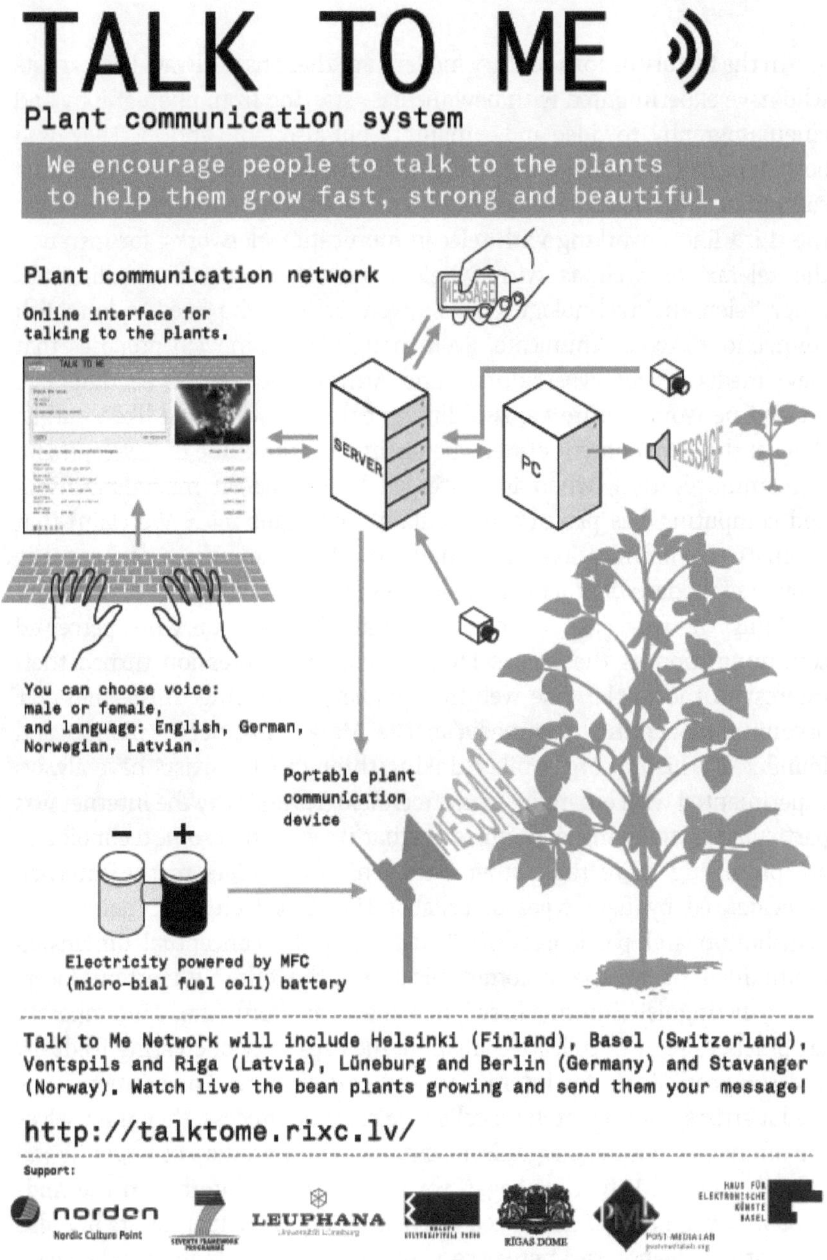

TALK TO ME))

Plant communication system

We encourage people to talk to the plants
to help them grow fast, strong and beautiful.

Plant communication network

Online interface for
talking to the plants.

You can choose voice:
male or female,
and language: English, German,
Norwegian, Latvian.

Portable plant
communication
device

Electricity powered by MFC
(micro-bial fuel cell) battery

Talk to Me Network will include Helsinki (Finland), Basel (Switzerland),
Ventspils and Riga (Latvia), Lüneburg and Berlin (Germany) and Stavanger
(Norway). Watch live the bean plants growing and send them your message!

http://talktome.rixc.lv/

Rasa Smite, Raitis Smits and Martins Ratniks, 'Talk to Me' project scheme and
postcard, 2012

In the history of 20th century modern art, there have always been artists who have experimented with new media – starting from photography and cinematography, to video and computers, but also radio and TV. They used both types of machines, according to Manovich – modern media and computers. Yet, there have also been artists who were more interested in the third line – working with telecommunication networks, for instance, the telefax, as well as with wireless, broadcasting and satellite and other 'telematic' technologies. These were artists who liked to 'establish connections', to communicate. Even though Lev Manovich proposes that 'new media is not cyberculture', and Armin Medosch states that 'net. art and network culture are two different things', we would like to argue that, in the development of new media art, this third line of development, telecommunication, when it converged with modern media machines and computing has played a particularly important role.[3] We claim that telematic communication was actually the key facet which conceptually converted modern digital media machines into 'new media'.

Thus, it was just as consequential that artists who perceived communication as the means for their creative expression turned their interest to the world wide web from its very beginning in the mid-90s, becoming pioneering 'new media' artists. Mark Tribe, net.art pioneer and founder of Rhizome.org, while thinking through why artists have always experimented with emerging media technologies and why the internet was particularly interesting for them, states that 'it seems, that some technologies are promising more than other ones. This fully refers to the Internet, as evidenced by new types of collaboration based creation, democratic distribution and participation.'[4] Thus, along the conceptual dimension maintained by telematic communications, the other important facets which distinguish (internet based) new media art from other contemporary art practices refer to collective creation, the capability of creating feedback and the possibilities for interaction and participation. Furthermore, new media artists not only prefer a collective creation process, they themselves are often also founders, organisers, curators and initiators of larger digital culture projects. When we began working with the internet in the mid-'90s, we were not just interested in creating our own art projects but also in creating collaborative networks, exploring the boundaries of cyberspace through streaming sound (as with Xchange – an internet radio network), establishing the RIXC media centre and running E-Lab locally in Riga, yet connected internationally through active networking. And often, when we talk about new media art practices, we forget that we should not just talk just about individual artwork, but about a whole set of processual activities within the field of new media art.

For instance, artist Marko Peljhan built Makrolab and proposed other independent communications infrastructures using alternative energy sources and autonomous communications systems, while RIXC suggested novel themes reflecting forthcoming trends such as 'locative media', 'ecology of the electromagnetic spectrum' and 'renewable futures', manifesting them through its annual Art+Communication festival public events. Thus, new media art practices, by exploiting the potential of collective creation, not only push the boundaries of art, but suggest a whole new paradigm in contemporary media-based art practices. It demands a redefinition of the borders of art, as well as the role of art within contemporary society, where today all functions and all layers of our social structures are influenced by new media technologies. Today technological convergence as well as a new perception triggered by new media no longer exist on the internet alone. Stereotypical expectations that new media will take over 'old media' have not happened. Instead convergence refers to all types of media technologies – as Guattari puts it 'we are witnessing the junction between television, telematics and informatics' which, for him, ushers in a 'post-media' age:

> The characteristic of suggestion, not to say of hypnotism, which qualifies television today will vanish. From that moment on, we can hope for a transformation of mass-mediatic power that will overcome contemporary subjectivity, and for the beginning of a post-media era that will be comprised of a collective reappropriation of the individual and an interactive use of machines of information, communication, intelligence, art and culture.[5]

Or putting it another way, when various important developments pioneered by early internet culture such as collective creation, sharing and social networking, are adapted and transformed by 'old' media, at the same time as their digitisation, we are entering a 'post-media' phase.

Post-Media Conditions in Art

If we analyse the impact of new media on 20th century art practices, we can detect a similar transformation process. Peter Weibel has argued that 'the new media were not only a new branch on the tree of art but actually transformed the tree of art itself.'[6] Artists who were working very actively with the world wide web in its early stages did not limit their explorations to it, but also followed other lines of media convergence. For instance, at the turn of the century, after a couple of years of collaborative explorations within 'acoustic cyberspace' we turned our interest to other communications technologies: in 2001 we worked with the RT32 Irbene radio telescope and satellite technologies together with radio astronomers, former Xchange network participants and sound artists; in 2003, it was 'locative media' that attracted our attention – an already hybridised technology that maintained connections between real and virtual worlds. In 21st century art practices, convergence, hybridisation and the mixing of both old and new media became increasingly relevant, replacing a primary focus on the internet. This particular state of contemporary media art practices, Weibel describes as the 'post-media condition': 'Consequently, this state of current art practice is best referred to as the post-media condition, because no single medium is dominant any longer; instead, all of the different media influence and determine each other.'[7] Weibel explains that the post-media condition is defined by two phases – the first is 'the equivalence of the media' and the second – 'the mixing of the media'. He writes:

> This mixing of the media has led to extraordinarily major innovations in each of the media and in art. Hence painting has come to life not by virtue of itself, but through its referencing of other media. Video lives from film, film lives from literature, and sculpture lives from photography and video. They all live from digital, technical innovations. The secret code behind all these forms of art is the binary code of the computer and the secret aesthetics consist of algorithmic rules and programs.[8]

From Weibel's perspective today 'all art is post-media art'. Yet, both Manovich when 'referring to new media objects' and Weibel when referring to the 'post-media condition in art' are actually sharing a similar view that, 'the secret code behind all these forms of art is the binary code of the computer and the secret aesthetics consist of algorithmic rules and programs.'

This perspective is very important for contextualising emerging techno-ecological art practices in terms of our thesis that they are dealing with ecological issues and dynamics, yet are rooted in new media. On the other hand, if bits and bytes in the post-media phase move into the background, and if the post-media condition in art is attenuated by an equality of media, then it becomes important to bring into the foreground another perspective based on conceptual and aesthetic values. Therefore, we return to the conceptual dimension of new media, and continue to highlight those features which once differentiated new media art from other contemporary art practices. Namely collective creation and process-based art practices, which were once key elements in new media art, and today have been reborn as important facets of post-media art. We claim that collective creation and process in the post-media phase of art will once again take over from result-based, individual artistic representations – with a few provisos. That we completely revise the notion of art as a process of individual creation, and the notion of the artist as a social outsider, and that we succeed in contextualising these new art practices within the existing field of art.

Both these features suggested by Weibel – 'equivalence of the media' and 'the mixing of the media' – can be found in emergent techno-ecological practices which we can thus refer to as post-media art. On the other hand, these new art practices are engaged in building a completely new domain which relates to renewable energy, sustainability and environmental issues. Their means of expression and communication are no longer primarily connected with media technologies, but can entail any material or media on an equal basis – yet, the message, the communication, the dialogue with society, becomes more important. This we are attempting within our recently established Renewable Network, in which artists are working together with scientists and local – urban and rural – communities, inviting people to participate in their artistic actions: to have a 'dinner with cows' and participate in 'weddings between art and agriculture' (Kultivator); to talk to the plants (RIXC): to grow edible plants in their windows, keep bees in the city (Christina Stadlbauer); become 'resilients' (Foam), to make edible solar cells from aronia juice (Bartaku); to build a bacteria battery from waste water (RIXC, LU scientists); or re-approach household traditions and learn local food production skills (Serde).

In relation to the activities of the Renewable Network artists, we can also trace a further line of development along the ecological axis. It is represented by the land art movement in the US during the late 1960s, and in the 1970s by Joseph Beuys' *7000 Oaks* action. On the one side these were manifestations of 'green' ideas which acted against the technological determinism of modern society. On the other hand, they were also process-based social actions – at least in Beuys' case, when he invited people to plant oak trees. And already in these cases, it became clear how powerful art can be in terms of reaching people's consciousness, introducing them to (r)evolutionary ideas and establishing dialogue.

However, as land art and ecological art were manifestations against the dominant development of modern technologies, for a very long time, they did not meet with the artistic exploration of technology. These trajectories have intersected more recently, and increasingly since the financial crisis of 2008, when artists who had been working with new media turned their interests towards environmental, energy and other sustainability issues, thus marking the beginning of the post-media era.

Art in the Post-Media Era: Re-Approaching Ecology

It now becomes clearer that there is no contradiction in the fact that artists who once explored the digital realm of 'unstable' media are today engaging with sustainability issues. Artists working with the internet in the '90s have used this media particularly intensely. Nineties net artists were interested in more than establishing communities and creative networks, creating net.art works or internet radio experiments. They also helped to shape the internet, pushing its boundaries and, last but not least, creating a new realm within digitally networked space. Having obtained such a deep experience of working with new media, it is unsurprising that today these artists are in the vanguard of building a techno-ecological perspective.

However, it is not that easy to make a shift from working with new media and information technologies to becoming engaged with environmental issues:

> Nobody likes it when you mention the unconscious, and nowadays, hardly anybody likes it when you mention the environment. When you mention the environment, you bring it into the foreground. In other words, it stops being the environment. It stops being That Thing Over There that surrounds and sustains us. When you think about where your waste goes, your world starts to shrink.[9]

When, after ten years of working with the internet and computers, we started to think about how such intensive work with machines that radiate electromagnetic fields influences us, our world started to shrink. The first artistic research project we did on the effects of electromagnetic radiation was *Skrunda Signal* and the exhibition Spectral Ecology (Riga, 2007), which we co-produced with Bureau d'Etudes, the French artists' collective, who helped us to create a map of electromagnetic radiation in Latvia. After interviewing scientists, biologists and physicians, who had spent ten years observing the Skrunda Radio Location station operating in Latvia, we came to the conclusion that even if 'electrosmog' is not very healthy, it's not that bad

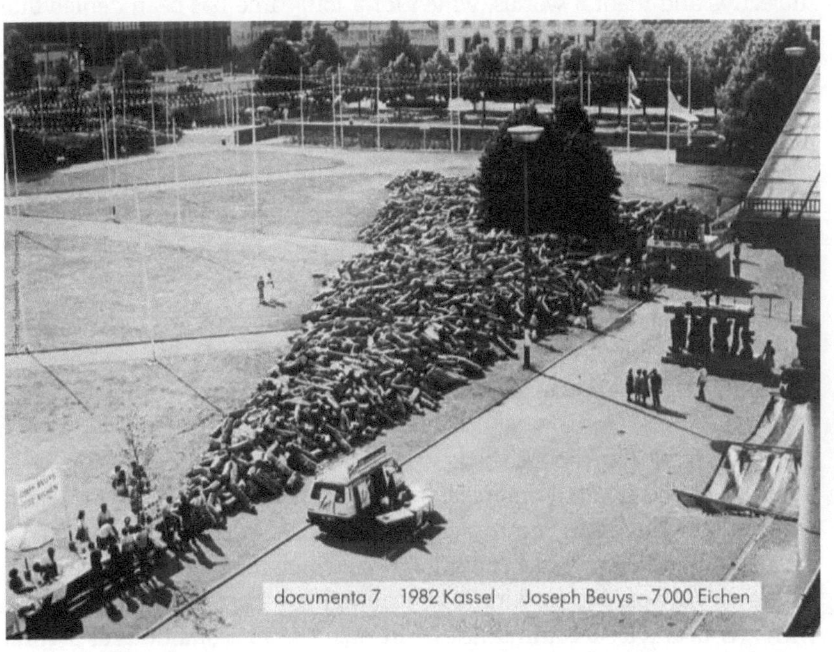

Joseph Beuys, *7000 Oaks*, Documenta 7, Kassel, 1982

either. In short, we won't all die, we can survive – but only if we can become adaptive. If we become 'resilients'. This was a very important conclusion for us: the idea that we can't simply reduce technologies to a traditional stereotype – that they are bad, they affect our health negatively, while nature is just good in all senses. Hence, we became aware of the complexity which techno-science has brought to our worlds, and that ecology does not automatically refer to nature and the environment, but that it is crucially important to integrate an ecological perspective in other fields as well – social, technological and cultural. Furthermore, ecology can also refer to subjective and mental worlds, which for a long time has been denied due to dominant techno-deterministic perspectives. Already back in the '90s, together with Eric Kluitenberg, we were discussing ideas relating to 'ecology without nature' – what 'data ecology' and 'media ecology' could be about. By referring to these early ideas, and wanting to combine his interest in 'deep technologies' with our artistic explorations of 'renewable futures', Eric Kluitenberg came up with the idea of 'techno-ecologies', largely basing it on Guattari's approach to ecology:

> More than ever today, nature has become inseparable from culture; and if we are to understand the interactions between ecosystems, the mechanosphere, and the social and individual universes of reference, we have to learn to think 'transversally'.[10]

The 'transveral' approach is the key; it is what artists from the Renewable Network are particularly interested in. In the Renewable Lab symposium which we organised in summer 2012 in rural settings throughout Latvia, we aimed to create unusual conditions – getting scientists out of their labs where they are used to working. By encouraging scientists to work together with artists and local communities – in such specific conditions as a 'rural lab' – we created a cultural context; situations in which scientists could see the impact of their research from a completely different perspective with regards to the materials they use, as well as how their work is perceived by local communities. For instance, when we experimented with the generation of electricity from the pond in our country house, young biologists made electrodes themselves by burning different types of materials – cotton (t-shirts), wood, papers – instead of using industrially manufactured ones. The role of artists, in this case, is to introduce an 'aesthetic paradigm' (Guattari) into the 'hard sciences'. Guattari advocates aesthetic paradigms, and not only in the arts, but in other fields as well, stressing that it is important, 'to develop and innovate, to create new perspectives, without prior recourse to assured theoretical foundations or the authority of a group, school, conservatory, or academy [...] Work in progress!' The 'creation of new perspectives', according to Guattari, refers to all fields; ecology being no exception, for it also needs to be approached from a radically new perspective. He distinguishes three complementary ecologies – environmental, social and mental. 'It is quite simply wrong', he wrote, 'to regard action on the psyche, the socius, and the environment as separate.'[11]

The 2008 crisis arrived in Latvia at the very end of the year, when we were taking down our large scale exhibition, Spectropia: Scientific Investigations and Artistic Explorations in Electromagnetic Spectrum, which followed the show Waves – Electromagnetic Waves as Material and Medium for the Arts. We realised that our new theme 'Energy', which we had planned for 2009, was particularly relevant. All confirmed funding for 2009 was cut for the RIXC organisation. Networking, which was our key tactic for surviving unstable times in the '90s, now came to the forefront. In 2009 we started building the Renewable Network, which unites artists with a mainly digital media background, but who have turned their interests to sustainability issues, approaching them from very diverse perspectives and combining different fields – art and agriculture, nature and technology, food production and open information systems, etc. These are very different topics, yet there is something common to them all – they share the same techno-ecological perspective. These emerging art practices are 'transversal' since they work on the edge of different disciplines, and 'post-medial' since they combine and mix different media. They also risk falling outside the boundaries of art. If they had not occasionally been exhibited in an art context, they would never have been considered art at all.

The Techno-Ecologies exhibition, which we co-curated under the theme and concept proposed and developed by Eric Kluitenberg, took place in Riga in 2011. Its intention was to create a material basis for the emerging Renewable Network initiative, and to put these emerging 'transversal' practices into an art context. In this exhibition, artist Bartaku introduced the way to make edible solar cells. But he is not willing to describe it in this way, because it is too narrow, too scientific; it says nothing about the cultural context nor the subject matter which involves relations between food and humans, since food is the primary energy resource needed by people, whereas sunlight is also important for all living bodies and plants on this planet. Calling his work *Temporary photoElectric Digestopians Worklabs*, Bartaku aims to show multi-layered meanings, which are included in an 'edible solar cell', its socio-cultural contexts and human inter-relations with the surrounding space. Bartaku combines photos inspired by mankind's struggle for energy. It shows the intimate entanglement of mind and body with the transformation of light into electrical and nutritional energy. The photos are made during co-creation work labs in which Bartaku invites the collaborators to make their own solar cells –from glass-based to edible ones.

Another work in the Techno-Ecologies exhibition exploring the relations between nature and technologies in urban environments, was Plantas Parlant's work by Popkalab. After investigating local water planning in the rich and fragile Dutch context, the group created a system capable of establishing relations between the human world and the vegetable world. They built a sonic sculpture formed by plants and electronic circuits where the contact between man and plant triggers sounds which poetically embody this relationship. The installation consists of several elements: controlling the flow of water in a closed circuit with different levels, inspired by the ingenious water management in the Netherlands; using vegetables pointing towards the possibility of food self supply; connecting plants through wires that capture the energy activity of bacteria and roots; exchanging the energy between plants and spectators, and making communication perceptible through audio signals caused by the interaction of the viewer. The installation functions as a vegetable electro-acoustic instrument.[12]

The socio-ecological approach was presented in The Toaster Project chronicles – an attempt by Thomas Thwaites to make an electric toaster from scratch – literally from the ground up. Thomas Thwaites is a designer, futurist and communicator, who strives to find new perspectives on technology. His design work examines how technology, science and economics interact with trends, fictions and beliefs, to shape our present society and possible futures. His toaster cost £11,87.54, and took him nine months to make. It's an electric appliance that disavows the infrastructure on which it relies. A convenient item that rejects the convenience of consumerism. A mass produced domestic product, 'manufactured' on a domestic scale. Its contradictions serve to highlight the amazing efficiencies of modern capitalism, but also to question our current trajectory.[13]

Other works in the Techno-Ecologies exhibition reflected upon social, technological and ecological sustainability issues. To mention just a few: Ingo Günther with his series of illuminated globes that deal with different interpretations of statistical data beyond geopolitical representations, including themes such as social development, life expectancy, the distribution of wealth; economic changes such as energy consumption and military conflicts. Artists from *Scenocosme* (Gregory Lasserre and Anais met den Ancxt) in their interactive artwork Phonofolium presented a living tree reacting to human touch by sound and voice. The artists who created this exhibit also included Danja Vasiliev and Julian Oliver who prefer to call themselves critical engineers. Last but not least, the show included Raul Nieves, Gerard Rubio, Jordi Bari from BlablabLAB (Spain), who demonstrated their self-made 3D printer, *be your own souvenir.*

Talk to Me – Post-Human / Post-Media Communication

However these emerging art practices are 'transversal', yet we claim them as 'art'. Even if it doesn't look like art, it can't be anything else. First, because of their methodologies. They are very different from the scientific approach. If science functions within strictly set borders, art creates the framework, context and borders by itself. Working with new media art, we have obtained experience not only in creating new perspectives, but also in building new (virtual, and hybrid) realms. As we have already mentioned, collective creation was the key, but so too is the diversification of forms. RIXC functions as a centre for new media culture, publisher of the *Acoustic Space* journal, organisers of an annual festival, and producers of workshops and symposia. Thus we have aimed at creating the context within which, together with our colleagues and others, we can explore new themes and develop new ideas. But as we are also artists, we have realised that often these ideas are better expressed through the production of artworks. Artworks are like 'shortcuts' – it is easier to communicate the relevant topics and new ideas to wider audiences. We, in RIXC, also work as an artists' collective. Our most recent artwork is *Talk to Me* – a plant communication network, which manifests and transforms our visions of 'renewable futures' by using artistic means of expression.

Talk to Me is a plant communication project and a networked installation, consisting of three main elements: on site – live growing bean plants in the exhibition space ('equipped' with web-cam, wi-fi connection and loudspeakers); online – an interface that allows people to 'talk' to the plants remotely (via the internet or by using their mobile devices); and networked nodes – other plants growing in other countries of Europe. The messages submitted by visitors (or online audience) are read aloud to the plants in the exhibition, and translated into the corresponding language for bean-plants in the network.

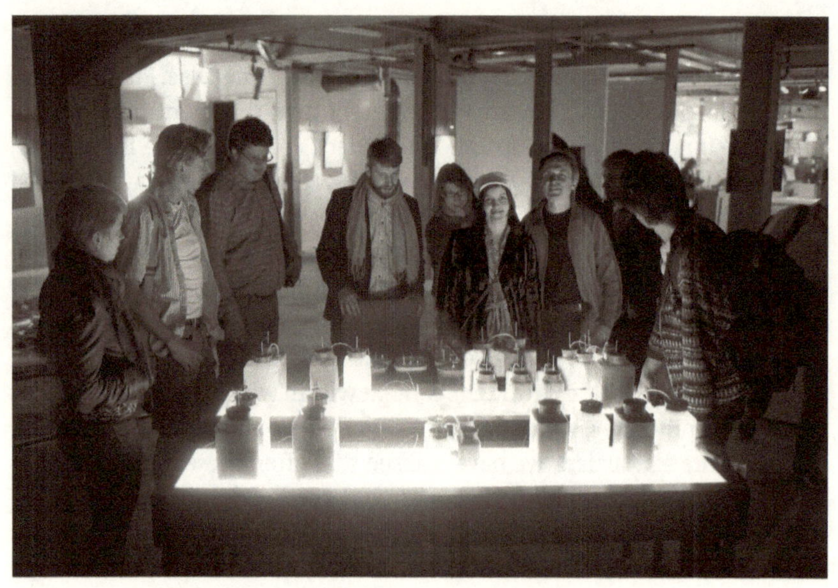

RIXC, *Bacteria Battery*, 2013. Photo by Boudewijn Bollmann

Talk to Me is a continuation of a participatory art campaign *Long Bean*, started in 2010, which was organised by RIXC and co-produced with the New Theatre Institute of Latvia (NTIL). It was based on the idea of 'grow[ing] your our own vegetables!' – we asked residents of Riga to grow different (edible) plants on their balconies, window sills and gardens, and contribute them to a collaborative installation in the RIXC Media space, which took place at the end of the summer of 2010 and was visited by thousands of people.

The *Long Bean* project had a twofold intent. First, the idea was to address the theme of 'food as an energy source'. Second was to explore the participatory art potential – we talked to people about their experience in urban and/or rural gardening, and we came to find that people actually do communicate with their plants. We reconfirmed something simple yet very true – everyone wants someone to talk to. Nowadays, even the scientists have performed various experiments in order to verify the old assumption that talking to plants makes them grow better. And so we started to develop an interface that allows us to talk to our plants remotely, for instance, while we are away from home.

In 2011, we developed the first version of the online interface (in English language) for the *Talk to Me* project. It was shown in a 4-month exhibition Gateways: Art and Networked Culture (curated by Sabine Himmelsbach) at the KUMU Museum, in Tallinn. About 10 thousand messages, submitted by visitors (and people online), were read out by text-to-speech software and played back on speakers to the plants during that summer.

This year (2012) we wanted to encourage people to talk to plants – but this time we wanted them to be able to use even more languages. We built a network of long bean plants that were located in different countries and talked different languages. The text-to-speech engine was updated, so that it could read and translate messages submitted via the internet or mobile devices, in order to read them aloud to long bean nodes in the plant-communication network. Growing installations were set up in all summer long at exhibitions in Riga (the Botanical Garden), in Ventspils (Latvia) and Basel (Switzerland), while one-day exhibits and presentations about the *Talk to Me* project took place in Helsinki (Finland), Lüneburg (Germany), Linz (Austria) and Stavanger (Norway). We are now working on *Talk to Me*'s future development. We are building a prototype for a self-sustainable 'plant-communication' device. It will be powered by a small-size bio-energy generator, which will produce electricity from bacteria living in soil and waste water. The 'bacteria-battery' technology will be developed in collaboration with Latvian scientists from the Biology Institute and the Solid State Physics Institute of the University of Latvia.

By experimenting with mixed media – next generation bio-energy technology, internet communication and growing plants – we are getting a step closer to renewable future scenarios. We are actually entering a new post-media era where previously separated networking systems – such as social, biological and electronic – now interrelate and intersect.

Conclusions

In contemporary media art, we are witnessing the transformation phase from new media to post-media. We argue that the post-media era is characterised not only by the ongoing convergence of modern media technologies, telematics and informatics, but also by an emerging new techno-ecological paradigm. Artists who were once internet pioneers are today among those engaging with sustainability issues – responding to dramatic techno-scientific transformations, which our planet is currently undergoing.

In post-media conditions artists are working transversally – in their quest for a sustainable future, they are working together with scientists as well as with local rural and urban communities to establish a dialogue with larger social groups. These emerging art practices, which are rooted in the '90s networking experience, explore the potential of collective creation, participatory culture and process-based artistic investigations. However, they have not yet succeeded in making their processual actions visible enough, since visibility is easier to obtain through individual artworks and exhibitions for which collective authorship is still an issue.

As far as it refers to mixed media and other materials which these emergent art practices are using, we can agree with Weibel, who claims that 'all art today is post-media art'.[14] Yet, if we talk about post-media conditions from the conceptual side, we see that the techno-ecological way of seeing the future has emerged, becoming a new trend in post-media art development. Beyond this, we would like to argue that the emerging techno-ecological art practices which the Renewable Network artists represent, suggest a paradigm shift from a techno-scientific to techno-ecological perspective, getting a step closer to renewable futures.

Footnotes

1   Eric Kluitenberg, 'Techno-Ecologies: Inhabiting the Deep-Technological Spheres of Everyday Life', in Rasa Smite, Eric Kluitenberg, Raitis Smits (Eds.) *Techno-Ecologies, Acoustic Space* #11, Riga: RIXC, Liepaja: LiepU MPLab, 2012, p.9.
2   Lev Manovich, *The Language of New Media*, Boston, MA: MIT, 2001, p.46.
3   Lev Manovich, *What is New Media: 8 Propositions*, 2001, http://manovich.net/new_media_images.html; Armin Medosch, interview by Rasa Smite for Creative Networks, e-mail interview, 2010.
4   Mark Tribe, Foreword, Lev Manovich, *The Language of New Media*, Boston, MA: MIT, 2001, p.x.
5   Felix Guattari, 'Towards a Post-Media Era', (1990), http://www.postmedialab.org/towards-post-media-era
6   Peter Weibel, 'The Post-Media Condition in Art', 2006, http://www.medialabmadrid.org/medialab/medialab.php?l=0&a=a&i=329
7   Ibid.
8   Ibid.
9   Timothy Morton, *Ecology Without Nature: Rethinking Environmental Aesthetics*, Cambridge, MA: Harvard University Press, 2007, p.1.
10 Felix Guattari, 'The Three Ecologies', *new formations*, No 8 Summer, 1989, pp.131-147
11 Ibid., p.34.
12 http://rixc.lv/11
13 http://rixc.lv/11/en/exhibition.artists/thomas.thwaites.html
14 Peter Weibel, 'The Post-Media Condition in Art', http://www.medialabmadrid.org/medialab/medialab.php?l=0&a=a&i=329 (2006)